When Mary and the Saints Spoke About the Anti-Christ

The logo I have made for the Legion of Mary, 2016

ANGELITA FELIXBERTO

WHEN MARY AND THE SAINTS SPOKE ABOUT THE ANTI-CHRIST

iUniverse books may be ordered through booksellers or by contacting:

iUniverse
1663 Liberty Drive
Bloomington, IN 47403
www.iuniverse.com
844-349-9409

ISBN: 978-1-6632-2468-2 (sc)
ISBN: 978-1-6632-2469-9 (e)

Print information available on the last page.

iUniverse rev. date: 06/30/2021

CONTENTS

Part 2: Saintly Prophecies about the Anti-Christ

INTRODUCTION

The book has two parts. The first one is about my experiences as a mystic vis-à-vis four Marian prophecies about chastisement and the second part is about saintly prophecies about the anti-Christ. My experiences might sound a little bit incredible but I was just pretty honest about it. I have been working on this book for a while now but I have also been taking some time off too because I just get too emotionally involved with it. It's like getting wounded in the battle and then taking some time off to heal and then on with the battle again. The wounds are just too real when I hear about what's going on in the Catholic Church today. I added more content to this book after I read about St. Malachy. I probably should write most of the content now like in a diary form to write my reflections but I have edited it according to the topic.

I ask everyone to suspend their disbelief and put themselves into the journey of what I am talking about.

The prophecies call us to comprehend what Mary and the saints are talking about, the grace of understanding divine revelation, a call to respond accordingly to what's being called upon.

My life as a mystic basically started when I had a dream about Mama introducing me to the Theotokos, a version of Our Lady of Perpetual Help. Since then, I have written down visions and I had to compile my notes. I have noted that the people in this age have somehow lost their connection with God because of the addiction to technology and the societal pride, secularism and plain stubbornness of people to recognize God. People have lost their moral standing to be in awe of such grace and to believe that miracles are indeed possible. Mystical visions are not to be used to satisfy people's curiosity, political ambitions, egoistic obsessions nor atheistic, agnostic or mere scientific challenges for understanding such grace although I understand the Church has to study if such undertakings were indeed authentic. The point is people need to focus on God, look for God, see God, not satisfy the overbearing inclinations of the human race to try to take control of this world without the faith in God. Thanks be to God and the Virgin Mary, for working on saving this planet, especially with a morally bankrupt leadership and society. God the Creator, whom I fondly call "Big Boss Daddy" have entrusted me with some skills needed to do such tasks. Everything I have done and I have to do is for the restoration of God's creation. I have said that from the very beginning. It is quite a teamwork though. Together with these four Marian prophecies and revelations from Saints, I get to understand the divine and the mystical realm of God's intention, purpose, design, and as what Jesus had already foretold from when He was on Earth, the Gospels written. The book has two parts, the first one is about my experience as a mystic vis-à-vis the Marian prophecies and two, what the Saints have said about the anti-Christ and apocalyptic revelations.

At some point when I realized this calling, I told God, I was the least qualified to do this task and I wrote some reflections but the answer to me was, "Nope. You're perfect." It was not that I am perfect and do not fall into temptations. It was that I was perfect for the job is what I understand. My temper, my personality, my feistiness and my closeness to God. All brings about a togetherness for perseverance. From the side of the Church, I would probably be just another delinquent rogue. There are other Marian apparitions but these four ones are the ones I was asked to understand and present. I chose three major saints and one blessed because of their apocalyptic prophecies.

PART 1

My Mystical Experiences

CHAPTER 1

My Childhood Days

When the author was about nine years old.

I was born in July of 1965. The year that the Second Vatican Council of the Catholic Church had just concluded. There were so many things that were going on at that time that was destined to change history. Today, there is a discussion about if the Vatican 2 is right or not. It was at the time when the Catholic Church dropped most of its orthodox ways and embraced new ways of doing things. It had become a stepping stone for more reforms which is countered by the conservative factions in the Church today. There is almost a schism in the Church where things stand. I have lived for over half a century now. Like an artist, I absorb almost every detail in my life, in high definition. I also realized that almost everything that has happened or is happening in my life is connected to some context like a solution to a puzzle.

I was born in Angeles City, Philippines. I migrated to the United States in 1992. I was a posthumous baby. My father died of stroke four months before I was born. He died a day right before my brother's second birthday and the story went on that my toddler brother was waiting for our Daddy to come home. Nineteen seems to be his number. He was born on July 19, 1919 and died on February 19, 1963. I would always hear my family talk about "Daddy" and I asked innocently then, "how come I don't have a Daddy?" One of my brothers would tease me "that's because we just found you out in a trash can and we adopted you!" That would always bring me into a tantrum. They never explained to me until later that my father passed away earlier, until at a time I could understand better. Almost everyone would just keep quiet when I started asking "What about my Daddy?"

My mother said I looked like almost a Caucasian baby when I was born! She kept a picture of this healthy, fair skinned, almost reddish haired baby and she told me it reminded her of me when I was born. She said that I was rather fair-skinned and my hair seemed reddish. She attributed it to the local water that may have stripped some elements or had some other chemical elements that affected hair color. Mama said that people were surprised that there's a baby at home because I hardly cried. We were also so poor then; I did not even have a crib.

I am the youngest of ten children. Two were unfortunately, blue babies, meaning they had the umbilical cord wrapped around their necks. They were Arturo and Maria. With my father's passing while my mother was still pregnant with me, I could just imagine all the grief, the stress, the worry, that she was then left with. There were eight children, including myself, whom she had to bring up all on her own. I must have been a fighter for survival even during when I was still being formed in the womb. All that emotional stress could probably have caused a miscarriage, even during midterm pregnancy, I would suppose. I was also born a breach baby. Breach baby means legs came out first instead of my head through the birth canal! Talking about dramatic entrance into this world!!!

I came to know later on that one of the reasons why my family moved from Angeles City to Manila was that our two dogs would seem to play around with someone or something invisible. Very strange and I guess kind of spooky to see two dogs frolicking with fun play with an invisible playmate! I must have already been two years old then when the family moved to the nation's capital, Manila. The family was originally from the Bicol Province, moved to province of Pampanga to get some fresher air from the very clannish in-laws and all that, and then my arrival brought the family right at the heart of the country.

My name really came from my birthplace: "Angeles," Spanish word for angels. My mother had asked me not to change my name, "Angelita" especially for the citizenship purposes when you get the only one opportunity to change your legal name. My godmother had a daughter named Mona and my mother and sisters liked this nice little girl that seemed to have this air of sophistication with her. She was a playmate to my brother. My family then handwrote "Mona" as my middle name in my birth certificate but the name never stuck with me because together with my third name, "Maria" it would be quite long to write my four names on the grade school pad. So supposedly, my official name is "Maria Mona Angelita." My nickname came from my mother's favorite actress, "Boots Anson-Roa" as suggested by my eldest sister. People thought that the name was rather cool odd and I got to be equally well known with it as my regular name. In college, I was one of those who pretty much just used my nickname and even after that.

The earliest I remember about my life was I think about five years old and I was supposed to take a nap. My mother laid down beside me herself to take a nap. Thinking my mother was already asleep, I slowly rose up and headed towards the stairs to play in the living room. In a very brief moment, I felt my shirt being tugged back into the bed. My mother pulled me back by my shirt and had me go back to napping. After that incident, I did not try to pull again much mischief, knowing that more than likely, I would just get caught again. That started my definition of right and wrong.

I remember the sights and sounds of the place like it was just from yesterday. A day in my life, consisted of observing and absorbing things. Perhaps before or after breakfast, while my mother prepared my siblings to go to school, I would watch the schoolchildren pass by. There were so many of them. I would watch them one by one or a group at a time pass by, heading to school, wondering when I myself would be going to school and have a school uniform. I thought that was kind of fancy.

Where we lived was a very strategic, convenient and colorful place. Several blocks away, with a very short jeepney ride was the University of Santo Tomas more popularly known as UST. UST is an old, pontifical, Catholic university. Through today, it is one of the largest educational institutions in the country. From our apartment, to the right, at what we called "North" was the Albert Elementary School where two of my siblings went. Further down is a primary school which I attended. The school was only up to the second grade. Between the primary school and our residence was a small city library. To me, this small place made of dark hardwood floors, and piles of book shelves with the strange combined scent of wood and paper, was some holy place that it required silence. This place, I guess, baptized my brother's love for books and a little bit of mine. I don't believe I really read books then, I just wanted to be able to borrow them. Being able to borrow them made me feel like I was old enough.

On this northern side, at the corner of the street was a bakery and convenience store owned by a Chinese guy. On the opposite side, the southern side, was another convenience store. This store was much bigger and perhaps a little busier. You just wait your turn on the counter that surrounds the store and the clerks, who more than likely were members of the same family, will come to you and get the item you want to purchase for you. Further down, a few blocks away is the Sampaloc Catholic Church where I had my first Communion. Behind our street was the local fresh market where the butchers cut and weighed the meat by kilos and then bagged in plastic. The fish vendors take the fish you point at, weigh it according to how much you wanted to buy, remove the scales and gills of the fish you point at, wrapped it in newspaper, hand it over to you and you pay. There were also all sorts of vegetables, grains, pantry stuff, and even artisan toys made for kids sold at the market. There were plenty of delicacies and beverages you can also munch on. A longer ride further away was the Central Market which to me was this gigantic place of merchants and tradespeople where children can get lost or kidnapped by Pinocchio's evil people in the city, never to be seen again, so I always held on tightly to my mother's hand whenever we go there.

The city itself was full of color, bustling with life. In our small street itself, only private transportation was allowed. On each end of our street was a main thoroughfare where plenty of *jeepneys* carried passengers to their destination. Oftentimes, when it rains, which was about half of the year, you may have to stay further away from the street curbs or wear the plastic boots, as the city's flood waters will soak you wet, as the jeepneys and cars pass by. This knee-high flood to me, can sometimes also steal your rubber flipflops if you're not too careful, letting it float for a little bit, before the tide from people's movements steal it away. These jeepneys, unique to the Philippines as it were domestically invented, were full of color. The *jeepneys* had like small flags or painted decorations inside, stickers, pictures, images, on them, on top of them, everywhere of them. As the years flew by or as I grew older, these *jeepneys* had a mixture of religious posted items like a driver's prayer, infant Jesus images and at the same time, also a couple of almost pornographic pictures of sexy women posted on the inside's ceiling or at the front part by the glass shields, side by side with the religious items. There were also "*calesas*" then, which was a horse-driven high carriage. I believe it was a little bit more expensive to take the *calesas* than the *jeepney*. It fared almost like a taxi or a pedicab. I always felt bad for the horses with their blinders, their mouths always dripping with saliva like they always needed water, and there was a bucket underneath the carriage, strategically located to catch the horse's wastes. Other than that, things kind of looked fine to me.

The story of my childhood pretty much opened up with this bustling capital district where the region's oldest pontifical university is located. People abound in the streets, day and night. Children played in the streets from the morning till dusk. Vendors passed by all day. The various modes of transportation, particularly the jeepneys ran through the streets.

Early on my mother taught me somehow that I was not a child of the streets. I had to choose my playmates very carefully. They had to be good, courteous, pleasant children and not those running around with uncouth, dirty little mouths. My mother was also kind of choosy with her friends.

At seven, I realized how a family works. I had plenty of older siblings who were already going to schools then. I realized the family sets the rules, and home is where home is.

One time, I encountered a troublemaker young girl, who challenged me to fight with her. She kept teasing me till I gave in and the boys around us could not wait enough for a catfight to happen. I don't remember who started it, but the next thing I knew, we were rolling on the ground, pulling each other's hair, and I got on top of her. Having lost the fight, she ran and ratted me to my mother that I was fighting with her. I told my mother that she provoked me, but my mother said, regardless of who started the fight, I was grounded, and not allowed to go out for a while. After that, I became friends with other kids who were much more pleasant.

My brother Felix, who is two years older than me is almost like a twin. I tended to follow him around with his friends. I guess it would be considered rather tomboyish if I liked playing and hanging around with the boys but his friends always treated me like a younger sister, almost like a princess, thus I enjoyed their company. We were playing a game where one would be on all fours on the ground and the other kids would jump over the "it" kid. When it was supposed to be my turn, the oldest of the boys, Dick, stopped the boys and told them not to have me do that. Such a hero!

I was thinking early this morning that I wanted to write about childhood: my childhood, the childhood as I have observed, the generational differences about childhood and so on and so forth. I thought the topic is too big to write in one single article. I would say that my childhood was a combination of so many things: tempered, exploratory, inherited passed on values and learning, and perhaps one which probably have been missed by generations after me: a carefree experience and exploration with nature. How many children in today's generation could say, they sang and danced under rain showers? How many children today would even know how tadpoles look like? How many would have had the chance to cross a shaking bridge made of bamboo sticks? Today's generation of children and childhood consists more of choosing responses in a pre-determined, pre-programmed computer software. Fancy designs of computer programs made to elicit responses from children and form and hone their skills. I did not have much luxury as a kid, or should I say, I did not have that kind of luxury at all. My total luxury was that, of creative imagination. "Pure imagination," as the great Willy Wonka sang.

When I was a kid, maybe six or seven years old, my toys were pretty much in my imagination. I had a magazine with like a silhouette of a baby, maybe about an inch size, and I pretended it was like a baby doll I would feed with a bottle of milk, like girls do with their dolls. My brother brought home some fancy glossy American magazines, and there would be pictures of kitchen or home designs with varying furnitures and I would pretend that I would see myself sitting in one of the seats in front of like a red-and-white chess design of tables and chairs in the kitchen. I also had plenty of coloring books, which always depicted a story. One was about Goldilocks, of whom I named my largest and walking doll after. The other coloring book was about how a Japanese family invented the paper lamp, with a candle inside a boxed sheet of paper. I shared a box of toys with my brother. The box was located at the far end of the bedroom by the door towards the balcony. The balcony was our playground and I can see the people passing by of whom I loved to watch. Watching people was one that kept me pretty preoccupied as a kid. Back to the toybox, it was filled with plastic figures of cowboys, animals and vehicles and such. These belonged to my brother. Our toys were mixed so we did not necessarily have to have them gender-identified, but I knew what was mine, what was his and what was ours. I remember there was a large seashell where you can hear the wind flowing through, like the sound of the ocean. We also had a pair of like that of a detective's magnifying glass and a pair of magnets that would make pencil shavings dance on a piece of paper. My mother and older siblings, would often buy a pair of toys for us and the mini version would be mine.

I also later on had like a collection of seven dolls with which I interchanged their actual dresses and my mother I believed, sewed some for them. Most of my dolls were Caucasian by the way. They were already fancy at that time. They opened and closed their eyes, their arms and legs were movable, some had plaster faces and they all had nice hair, one or two of which I would turn into a braid.

My favorite one, was perhaps the only one I named, Goldilocks. I doubt if she had batteries but her legs were designed to be movable that she can put one foot ahead of the other, and it would be like you were walking a child. I didn't have Barbie dolls. At all. My dolls were almost all child-like and wore childlike clothes like a nightwear. One seemed fancy enough to be like an older child but it did not depict a fancy-shaped Barbie. Looking back, I think what I enjoyed the most was just the innocence of being a child. Perhaps as if it was meant to be.

When I watched the children from my balcony, I think there was just a very slight tinge of envy. I was the last one to go to school, as the youngest child, so as my mother did the housework while my siblings were in school, I had to stay at home and be under the watchful eye of my mother. I tried to play outside once and learned soon enough that I had to pick my playmates very carefully.

As much of what's outside home reflected decade 70's, the people themselves reflected the decade: the polyester blouses, the miniskirts, the false eyelashes, the psychedelic clothing with those busy, busy designs; the elephant pants, the squarish high heels or what they called "clogs."

What was interesting to me was that our residence had street names from characters of the book "Noli Me Tangere" by the Philippine national hero, Jose Rizal. The title of "Noli Me Tangere" was taken from the Easter scene when Mary Magdalene tried to approach Jesus and he asked not to be touched yet for He has not come back to the Father.

CHAPTER 2

A Religiously Zealous Kid

I still remember my first Holy Communion like it just happened yesterday. The details are very fresh in my mind. I got to wear a very nice girly white dress with some ribbon frills, a little round white lacey veil, new black shoes and white socks with lace on the edges. The walk towards the church took a few blocks but I was pretty excited and was quite nervous along the way. A few months before, my mother gave me my first catechism books where and when I first learned about angels and about God, and that I have to be a good kid to please God.

The church we went to, to me was huge and there were lots of people. So, there I was at one point, standing by the altar, in line to receive the Holy Eucharist from the priest. The Holy Mass was long. I didn't really quite understand it at seven years old. All I knew was that the priest gave a sermon that we should be good people, and good Christians. The people sat, stood up, knelt and sat again several times. Finally, I was there to receive the Holy Communion. I clasped my hands in prayer and received God the very first time.

My family was a very devout Catholic. As a family, we prayed the Angelus every six o'clock at night. Never missed one. We said the prayer before meals. Sundays were always a church day.

At home, we had a small altar with a statue of Christ the King, St. Lucy and St. Jude Thaddeus. I did not know why but my mother would always pray a novena at around 3 o'clock in the afternoon. I was later taught that, according to the elders, that was the time when Jesus breathed his last. Three o'clock in the afternoon therefore signified a holy hour, a couple of decades even before the Divine Mercy adoration came into being.

I would see my mother kneel down in front of the small altar which was the top of a small shelf but decorated with the finest crocheted piece. She would then open up and go through a couple of pages on her novena booklet and I believe she also prayed the rosary. There was a couple of small New Testament Bibles. We were allowed to read it although of course, it was pretty much beyond my comprehension at that time. At times, I would kneel down beside my mother and just mumble pretending and imitating her.

At six o'clock, when everyone would have arrived from school or work, we would all kneel down in front of the small altar and pray the Angelus. I believe I was already somehow familiar with it at that time.

Mama introduced the Virgin Mary to me in an odd way. She said that a cat laid on Mary's garments and since she did not want the cat disturbed, she had her garments cut instead. It was a very simple story but had connected with me very well since I am very fond of cats.

Whenever we would go downtown, my mother would make it a point to attend the Mass first at the local church, the Church of the Black Nazarene. It seemed like every hour or two, they hold a Mass.

The Church of the Black Nazarene was more popularly known as the Quiapo Church. It was quite the Grand Central. Every year, tens of thousands of pilgrims would join the procession of the Black Nazarene. It is a statue of Jesus kneeling down as He carries a black cross. Jesus is dressed in a dark plum red garb. The long, very crowded procession expressed true and deep faith in God among the devotees. They believed that veneration and touching the holy statue of Jesus would bring answers to deeply felt supplications.

So, my mother always brought me to attend first the Holy Mass once we get downtown. This was before we did anything else. I still would not understand much about the Holy Mass then because to me the priest at the altar was just mumbling or rambling. As a kid, I usually stared at the statues of saints inside the church. I noticed the statues of the saints had long beards, tall noses, usually with a book or a staff and with long garments. The saints all looked like foreigners to me. I thought that was how holy people must have looked like a long time ago. I was also not too fond of the incense inside the church. The smell of the incense that would fill up my nostrils was kind of weird. I did not think it was bad but neither was it good. It was just a smell I associated with the church.

During the Mass, I liked knowing when to do the signs of the cross and me rushing to do it. At that time of the Holy Communion, people would move towards the altar and kneel at the cushioned kneel paddings in front of the rails. To me, as a kid, that meant that the long sermon of the mumbling priest was over. Most of the time, I listened anyway not that I understood. If I did not understand the priest, my mind would just drift off lazily somewhere.

As we went in, through and out of the church, there was no way we can escape running into the vendors who filled the church. It felt like that they were the living structural parts of the church. The church building would not be the church without all these people, including all these hustling and bustling vendors some within but mostly around the church. They were vendors of all trades and kinds: flowers, candles, lottery tickets, abortifacients, yes, herbal abortifacients in unmarked, solid brown glass bottles. It's almost like you can hear Jesus saying "Stop turning my Temple into a marketplace!" but where people were, vendors were there too.

For the enterprising religious, there were also women who would say rosary prayers for busy people in exchange for money. Very enterprising indeed. My mother never believed in them though because she prayed her own rosary at the start of the day and/or at the end of the day. There were also people who sold human-shaped candles aimed at using almost voodoo-like prayer intentions for particular people. There were also women who would pin religious medals especially on kids and then ask for payment. It was such a hassle returning the medal that might as well just pay for it. Yes, the church was very much a den of thieves. The church administrators could not really do anything about it. They would try to restrict the vendors in the church. The next day they were back in. It was almost futile to even try. The hustle and bustle of the common crowd made the church what it was to the common people though.

Of course, there were the devotees who would pray from the back of the church to the altar at the front, on their knees. There were the prayers for the sick or dying family member, the prayers to find a job or win the lottery. For the aging women past 25 years old, to find a husband. You could see people so engaged in their novenas and rosaries, sometimes even during the Mass. There was also a time when a woman dressed in white with a blue sash, like the garb of Our Lady of Lourdes, climbed the altar of Our Lady and started singing, even while the Mass was going on. It took a little time before the church security could get the woman down from the altar, hopefully back to planet Earth too. Maybe she was truly moved and inspired. The people were more nonchalant with it though. It was almost like New York Central with where sometimes people ignored the extraordinary things because it seemed normal in a crazy metropolis. Despite all that craziness though, devotion to Jesus of Nazarene, found its way and resided in people's hearts unmoved and permanently in existence.

It was also around this time that Mama told me about Jesus holding up his two fingers. Mama told me that that's actually

13

when the Messiah will be back. It was just our secret. Mama repeated it again during breakfast. I thought nobody will believe me so I kept it within me.

My first getting to know about Jesus was through this picture of "The Eye" on a clothes dresser, across the dining table in our tiny apartment back then. I always thought that He was looking at me and was following me around. The picture or the painting of Jesus was made that way that from whichever angle you look at it, it would seem like He was looking at you. So, there was one time or maybe a couple of times, I would swing my head back and forth to the left and right side of Jesus' picture to double-check if He was still looking at me! I think I would kind of run back and forth side to side too to check if He was still looking at me! I believe I was around six or seven years old then.

I guess I should call it "emotional connection." My first emotional connection with Jesus was during Holy Week actually. Back then, Holy Week was seriously, seriously observed! Of course, the Palm Sunday was well celebrated with some even fancy coconut branch with its leaves weaved artistically. Come Holy Monday though, we kids were taught to seriously observe the Holy Week, meaning less boisterous laughter and less running around. We were supposed to observe a calmer, quieter demeanor. Holy Week back then in the Philippines was the time when all these old movies about Jesus' passion, death and resurrection were televised. There was one program my mother watched which was, if I remember correctly, was about "The Seven Last Words." I still remember there were two or three people, one of them was a priest and the program was quite long, I was just in and out of the room, I would peek at the TV every now and then. I believe around the seventh words, either I stayed in the room or my mother called me to stay in the room. There was this huge, I think almost life-size crucifix and by the last word or by 3 PM, Jesus' head was supposed to bow down upon His death. I watched Him at that moment and I believe I felt sorry for Him, thinking like He was the ultimate underdog. It was at that very moment though that there was this emotional connection that would stay with me permanently. And then my mother told me to watch the sky because she said, every Good Friday at 3 PM, on Jesus' death, the sky or the clouds would get dark and that never fails. I believe it had. There were also some other things my mother pointed out to me from the other TV programs. She said the curtains in the Temple, I believe would rip, because He was indeed the Son of God. So, I watched those details in a very absorbed way. I believe there was lightning and thunder and then the curtains ripped and then it rained. I think that was the scene I remember. I believe I asked Mama then, "how did she knew all that?"

CHAPTER 3

My "Lost in The Temple" Story

I just found this image of the altar at the Church of the Black Nazarene. The two stained glass windows on both sides, just look too familiar to the nth degree. I always loved these stained-glass windows and as a kid, the resurrected Christ always drew my attention. It's almost very comforting.

The Church of the Black Nazarene or Quiapo Church, among perhaps thousands of its weekly devotees was quite too familiar and was the setting of my then growing devotion to Jesus. At the back of the Church was a statue of Christ enclosed in a glass case or like a glass tomb. I think they call it *"hinulid."* I later wondered why I have this affection for a "dead Christ" or Christ in the Holy Sepulcher but I thought it was more of like an inexplicable affection. Hundreds of people probably pass through the image on a daily basis and would wipe their handkerchief on His feet which was extended outside the glass, or by His head, or just wipe it on the glass case and then utter their prayers. The weird thing about me though is that I would stare at His face and to me it looked like His eyes were just kind of like in a half-asleep mode. It's like He didn't look dead to me. I believe Mama noticed that that I would stare at Jesus' face intently and one time she told me that that's how my Daddy looked like when he goes to sleep. I believed her thinking that my father had a taller nose.

It was also right there by Jesus' enclosed statue, that my mother thought she lost me in the Church! I think I was perhaps around 12 years old. I was with my mother and sister Ruby, and maybe I thought they noticed me taking off or that I may have gotten swept away by the crowd but I actually fell in line with the people towards Jesus' enclosed statue. I think my mother somehow panicked for a little bit wondering where I was until I waved or yelled, "Mama!" I think there was a big relief for her and I cannot remember if she and my sister joined the line instead or they just waited for me at the exit of the line.

CHAPTER 4

Mama: Also, A Mystic?

Mama always taught us, "God will provide." This has been like our family mantra. It's like the very core of our faith. It's like a mustard seed that Mama planted in our brains since we were kids and the richness yielding from that tree will be like our source of bounty. Just simply true enough, Divine Providence has always carried us through.

When I was between age 10 and 12, Mama bought two gold watches. One was for her; one was for me. They were the same brand and it looked exactly the same except for the face of the watch. I believe the face of her watch was more gold, mine was more like yellowish gold. I was kind of proud or flaunting it around that Mama and I had like matching new watches. Mama told me not to flaunt it around. I was kid, I didn't really understand then.

For a while, as I have realized that almost everything in my life has or had a significance, I have been thinking about those pair of matching watches Mama and I had. In interpreting the Marian prophecies, particularly, one of the abilities I recognize I have is to see the connections in time about details and its meaning. There is also something that connects me, physically, in terms of some details, to the Marian prophecies. This also involves finding St.

John Paul 2 in his constant appearances and at some point, led back to me, for connection.

There was a time during her youth when foreign missionaries had come to the ancestral provincial area. Encouraged by relatives who were impressed with the work ethic of the missionaries, Mama agreed to convert to their faith. To and from the place, they had to take a boat ride. On the way home from the baptismal event they joined, the sea suddenly became tumultuous. It was a very frightening experience, we presumed from how she was talking about it. In the middle of all that fear that the boat might capsize, Mama said she saw Mary's apparition above and at the front of the boat. Mary appeared as Our Lady of Miraculous Medal. Mama said she particularly remember Mary's arms outstretched on the side with like rays of light emanating from her hands. Mama said she begged Mary to save their lives and she promised to come back to Catholicism. The waves must have calmed down a lot and they sailed back to safety.

Decades before I was born, my native country fell under the Japanese occupation during World War II. Words were sent out that some local people who wanted to seek favor from the Japanese forces will report some names of people treacherous to the Japanese. I believe Mama and Daddy were only betrothed at that time. To be safe, both Mama and Daddy changed their names and fled to safety. Mama used the name "Lourdes" and my father's middle name, "Avila," thus her name became "Lourdes Avila." My father changed his last name from "Gonzales" to our current last name and kept it as is. Given the change and that Gonzales is a very common last name, it would be very difficult to trace the patrilineal side. Years later, I was born as a posthumous baby. My father died when I was five months in the womb. At nine years old, my mother "consecrated" me to Mary, basically introducing me to the novena of Our Lady of Miraculous Medal. The same Lady that saved their lives when the boat was about to capsize.

Mama, I believe was also a mystic, meaning she had supernatural visions. One time, when she accompanied one of my sisters for an out-of-town college enrollment, my sister that night had gotten a fever. The fever must have been brought about by the sudden change of temperature since that city was at a higher altitude and much colder. My mother was pretty worried that through the night, they might find it very difficult to go to a hospital, if the high fever persists. While half-awake, she saw her deceased spiritual director preparing a face towel in his hands and putting it on my sister's forehead. Miraculously, my sister's fever broke through the night and was quite back to normal in the morning. Mama later recalled her vision to us when they returned home. My mother's spiritual director died quite like a martyr for the Church. He was in charge of the Church treasury and a man went to rob the Church's money. He slit the priest's throat. I never met him in person, but he was like a member of our family almost from the stories that Mama spoke of about him. The Church then undertook some changes for better protection of its clergy and matters.

One memorable experience I had was that when Mama was already sick with cancer then, I visited her at the hospital. My sister had left the room so it was just Mama and myself. I saw Mama moving her smallest finger. I remember she told me stories when I was a kid about that. I think it may also have something to do with when people wake up from a coma, the first sign of life is usually through the fingers. Slowly, Mama opened up her eyes and looked at me very intently. Her eyes looked very, very strange because the iris seemed detached from the pupil. I have never thought that that was possible for human eyes. She looked at me very intently for a few minutes. There was a mixed feeling in me about I did not know exactly what to think right at that moment. It was a mixture of wonder and some fear because it was very strange to me. She then closed her eyes again and went to relax and go back to sleep. Realizing she wanted to go back to sleep, I came out of the room and looked for my sister.

I remember Mama always telling me before, "Trust me because the Lord is guiding me." To me, I had no questions about that. Anyone who loves his or her mother would trust her completely. The experience of her looking at me with those strange eyes, I later reflected on it is like her passing on her legacy to me as being a mystic. It seemed like a forewarning that I will become a mystic myself. When Mama passed away a few months after, I was 33 years old then. To me, it was significant because Jesus died at 33 years old, only here it's the reverse, I lost my mother. My brother gave the eulogy and what was memorable to me was the line he wrote: "we may be lacking plenty of material things, but we were never lacking of a mother's love." In the invitation to her memorial mass, we had it written there, "God will provide. – Mama." We thought that that would be our best, perfect tribute to her.

CHAPTER 5

The Sign from the Dreams

Before I had my first mystical vision of Mary, I dreamt about my mother. She brought me right in front of a life-size image of Mary with the baby Jesus. We stood right in front of it with Mama on my left-hand side. I recognized the icon as Our Lady of Perpetual Help. I noticed and asked why was Mary's veil black? I am more familiar with the icon though with Mary having like a dark blue veil. When I woke up, I researched about the icon on Google and found out that it was a real-life 15th century Marian image.

The Byzantine Icon: Our Lady of Perpetual Help

This 15th-century Byzantine icon is known by one of the Roman Catholic titles of the Blessed Virgin Mary, Our Lady of Perpetual Help, also associated with the same Marian apparition. The image, as popular legends claim, is a true copy of a painting by Saint Luke using the meal table of the Holy Family in Nazareth. In the Eastern Orthodox tradition, it is identified as a Hodegetria icon. It is an iconographic depiction of the Theotokos (Virgin Mary) holding the Child Jesus at her side while pointing to Him as the source of salvation for humankind. The Virgin's head usually inclines towards the Child, who raises his hand in a blessing gesture. A Hodegetria icon is considered to be a miraculous imprint of the Virgin Mary both in the Latin and Orthodox icons. It is a common belief that many Hodegetria icons have similar origins of Lucan legends. There are many great stories of miraculous appearance of the Theotokos icon.

In 1499, the icon was said to have been stolen from the Keras Kardiotissas Monastery in Crete. It was in the private possession of a Roman merchant and his family. It was later transferred to the Church of San Matteo for its first public veneration. It remained there for three centuries and was popularly called the Madonna di San Matteo.

In 1798, as part of the French Revolutionary Wars, French troops under Louise-Alexander Berthier occupied Rome and demolished several churches including the Church of San Matteo which housed the icon. The Augustinian friars rescued the icon and took it to the nearby Church of St. Eusebius, then later set it up on a side altar in the Church of Santa Maria in Posterula.

In 1855, the Redemptorist priests purchased Villa Caserta in Rome along the Via Merulana. They converted the property into their headquarters. Decades later, in response to Pope Pius IX's invitation to set up a Marian house of veneration in Rome, they built the Church of St. Alphonsus. Without realizing it, they have established themselves on the location where the Church of San Matteo and shrine of the once-famous icon used to stand.

In 1865, Pope Pius IX sent a letter to the Father General of the Redemptorists, ordering that the image be once again publicly venerated in the new church of Saint Alphonsus.

A year later, the Redemptorist Superior General gave one of the first copies of the icon to Pope Pius IX. This copy is preserved in the chapel of the Redemptorists Generalate in Rome. The icon underwent restoration by the Polish painter Leopold Nowotny (1822-1870). A copy given to the Pope is preserved in the chapel of the Redemptorists Generalate in Rome while the original icon remains under the care of the Redemptorist Fathers at the Church of St. Alphonsus. The latest restoration work was undertaken in 1990.

Another year later, Pope Pius IX granted the image its Canonical Coronation along with its present title. The icon was entrusted to the Redemptorist priests, by the Holy See, to protect and propagate a Marian religious work of art. Due to the instruments of the Passion of Jesus Christ present on the image, the icon has become known as the "Virgin Theotokos of the Passion" in the Eastern Orthodox Church traditions. The feast day of the image is celebrated on June 27, with novena devotions held every Wednesday.

In the years under Pope Pius XII's Pontificate, the image was designated as the national Patroness of the Republic of Haiti and Almoradi, Spain.

In 1999, Pope John Paul II issued a canonical coronation for a similar image in Jaworzno, Poland.

Theotokos of Tikhvin

Another story of the icon of Theotokos was about the Theotokos of Tikhvin, one of the most celebrated Orthodox Christian icons said to be written by St. Luke the Evangelist. According to tradition, in the 5th century, the icon was transferred from Jerusalem to Constantinople. It was placed in a church especially built for it. The same traditions have been conflated with the Tikhvin icon of the Hodegetria type. Some art historians prefer a date of 1300 and a Russian artist. It closely refers to a tradition that the icon miraculously appeared, hovering over a lake, in Russia near Tikhvin in 1383.

Since the 14th century, the icon was held in Tikhvin. Later, the Tikhvin Assumption Monastery was founded to host the icon. In 1941, during World War II, the German troops occupied Tikhvin for a month. They looted the monastery and in particular, took the icon to Pskov, and in 1944, transferred it to Riga. A Russian Orthodox bishop from Kolka and later Bishop of Riga, John (Garklavs), eventually took the icon out of Russia for safety. In between 1949 and 2004, the icon remained at the Holy Trinity Orthodox Cathedral in Chicago, Illinois, United States. In 2004, it was returned to Tikhvin, Russia by his adopted son, Fr. Sergei Garklavs of Chicago. The icon was kept at the Tikhvin Assumption Monastery, where it was kept prior to 1917. Most of the icon, except the exposed skin of Jesus and Mary (the two faces and necks, both set of hands and the feet of Jesus), is normally covered by a frame of precious metals and riza jewels.

Theotokos of Kazan

The original icon of Our Lady of Kazan was brought to Russia from Constantinople in the 13th century, according to tradition. The icon disappeared from the historical record for more than a century after the establishment of the Khanate of Kazan (c.1348). The recovery of the icon was described in the Metropolitan Hermogenes chronicle, written at the request of Tsar Fodor in 1595. According to this account, after a fire destroyed Kazan in 1579, the Virgin appeared to a 10-year-old girl, Matrona, to whom she revealed the location of the icon. The girl told the archbishop about her dream but she was not taken seriously. However, after two repetitions of the dream, the girl and her mother recovered the icon on their own on July 8,1579. It was buried under a destroyed house where it had been hidden to save it from the Tatars.

Russian military commanders Dmitry Pozharsky (17th century) and Mikhail Kutuzov (19th century) credited the invocation of the Virgin Mary through the icon with helping the country repel the Polish invasion of 1612, the Swedish invasion of 1709 and Napoleon's invasion of 1812. The Kazan icon achieved immense popularity. There were nine of ten separate miracle-attributed copies of the icon around Russia.

On the night of June 29, 1904, the icon was stolen from the Kazan Convent of the Theotokos in Kazan where it had been kept for centuries. The building was later blown-up by communist authorities. Thieves apparently coveted the icon's gold frame, ornamented with many valuable jewels. Several years later, the Russian police were able to apprehend the thieves and recovered the frame. The thieves originally declared that the icon itself had been cut to pieces and burnt. One of the thieves though eventually confessed that it was housed in a monastery in the wilds of Siberia. The Russian police refused to investigate, believing it to be a fake. They believed that it would be very unlucky to venerate a fake icon as though it were authentic. The Orthodox Church interpreted the disappearance of the icon as a sign of tragedies that would plague Russia after the image of the Holy Protectress of Russia had been lost. The miseries of the Revolution of 1905, as well as Russia's defeat in the Russo-Japanese War of 1904-1905 was blamed by the peasantry to the desecration of her image.

Theories of speculation ran around for several years. After the Russian Revolution of 1917, there was a speculation that the original icon was in fact preserved in St. Petersburg. Reportedly, an icon of Our Lady of Kazan used in processions around Leningrad fortifications during the Siege of Leningrad (1941-1944) during World War II.

Another theory proposed was that the Bolsheviks had sold the image abroad. The Russian Orthodox Church did not agree with such theories. The history of the stolen icon between 1917 and 1953 is unknown. In 1953, Frederick Mitchell-Hedges purchased an icon from Arthur Hillman. Although the status of the original Kazan icon remained disputed, Cyril G.E. Bunt concluded that while it was copy of the original icon, it was nevertheless the original icon from 1612. He said that "it is the work of a great icon painter of the 16th century …the pigments and the wood of the panel are perfectly preserved as exhaustive X-ray tests have proved, and have mellowed with age.[1]" The icon was exhibited at

---

[1] "Our Lady of Kazan." Wikipedia. Retrieved from https://en.wikipedia.org/wiki/Our_Lady_of_Kazan. May 12, 2021.

the World Trade Fair in New York in 1964-1965. On September 13, 1965, members of the Blue Army of Our Lady of Fatima spent the night in veneration of the icon in the pavilion in New York. The icon was eventually bought by the Blue Army from Anna Mitchell-Hedges for US$125,000. In January 1970, the icon was enshrined in Fatima, Portugal.

In 1993, the icon from Fatima was given to the Vatican. Pope John Paul II had it installed in his study, where he venerated the icon for eleven years. "It has found a home with me and has accompanied my daily service to the Church with its motherly gaze," he said. John Paul II wished to visit Moscow or Kazan so that he himself could return the icon to the Russian Orthodox Church. However, the Moscow Patriarchate was suspicious that the Pope might have other motives. He thus presented the icon to the Russian Church unconditionally in August 2004. On August 26, 2004, it was exhibited for veneration on the altar of St. Peter's Basilica and then delivered to Moscow. On the next feast day of the holy icon, July 21,2005, the icon was received by Patriarch Alexius II and Mintimer Shaymiev, the president of Tatarstan, in the Annunciation Cathedral of the Kazan Kremlin.

The icon is now enshrined in the Cathedral of the Elevation of the Holy Cross. The cathedral was part of the Convent of Theotokos which was reestablished as a monastery in 2005, on the site where the original icon of Our Lady of Kazan was found. Plans are now underway to make the monastery's other buildings into an international pilgrimage center.

Other churches were built in honor of the revelation of the Virgin of Kazan. Copies of the image were displayed at the Kazan Cathedral of Moscow (constructed in the early 17th century), at Yaroslavl and at St. Petersburg.

CHAPTER 6

When Mary Spoke

The experience was truly amazing and overwhelming that I have thought over and over again at that time, "Mary, the Mother of God? I am talking to Mary, the Mother of God?" I thought, "Who would believe that?" I thought that she was truly sublime, without a bad bone in her body, just radiating with purity. It was truly a vision. I would not have had merely created that vision.

The experience was truly amazing and overwhelming that I have thought over and over again at that time, "Mary, the Mother of God? I am talking to Mary, the Mother of God?" I thought, "Who would believe that?" Much more so I thought that talking to Mary seems to be like talking to an ordinary person. The conversation was very down-to-earth and the relationship is so real, with no pretenses. It's like talking to your mother or talking to your friend which came very natural for me because Mama was like my best friend. We're almost like sisters. We have a bond. I also felt that bond with Mary.

Mary and I spoke about many things. She told me about things that were supposed to happen. Sometimes we just chatted. A sample of this conversation was on April 19, 2017 when I wrote the following notes. I tried to link them with the various events that had occurred.

- **Brazil soccer team** *(Brazilian soccer team's flight crashed, 2016)*
- **Where did Nelson Mandela come from?** South Africa
- **Nelson Mandela smiling** *(2018 was his centennial)*
- **Racism will get intense** *(Trump administration especially towards 2020)*
- **More corrupt political government** *(Venezuela economic sanctions via Trump's executive order - President Madura's disregard for law issue, August 2017; anti-corruption rally in Israel vs. Netanyahu)*
- **Being eyed by Boko Haram**
- **Star of David, also looks like Filipino Christmas lantern shape** *(Israel, Philippines)*
- **Southern Philippines** *(Battle of Marawi occurred on May through October 2017)*
- **Several images of Mary like Mediatrix with blue cloth, white cloth, with 12 starts, with a crown, with a baby**
- **Our Lady of Prompt Succor**
- **St. Jude Thaddeus**
- **St Anthony of Padua** *(Parish where Pastor was transferred to)*
- **St Martin de Porres**
- **St. Mother Teresa of Calcutta** "Bread, especially for the hungry children…"
- **What do you call the Order of St. Anthony de Padua?** Franciscan. *Story about baby Jesus in St. Anthony's arms*
- **Cinco de Mayo, Rio de Janeiro**, Olympics = summer olympics
- **Madrid, Spain** - President *(August 2017 ISIS bombing of Barcelona, Spain---> Madrid)*
- **Targeted King** - controversial
- **Queen/Princess in Spain** (Queen of Jordan visited the US March 2017. More?)
- **2017** - sports game - soccer?

- **August 2017** - St. Louis Missouri, the arc
- **Racial protests of immense proportions** = *(Trump administration. Triggered by the George Floyd incident, global racial protests)*
- **Virginia Beach, Virginia** *(Charlottesville, VA?)*
- **US Navy** *(trouble with periodic sea mishaps, coronavirus incident, 2020)*
- **Warships** *(Additional troops to Afghanistan, August 2017)*
- **Samuel Gordon**
- **USS Battlestar** *(7th Fleet, US Navy, etc. - being checked for mishaps)*
- **Why did I write Gaudium et Spes as a note?**
- **Female Navy Admiral** = key in making decisions *(Secretary of the Navy, female)*
- **White knight on a brown horse**
- **Axe of the axeman**
- **What constellation is the archer, Aries?** *(August 21 eclipse noted)*
- **Cairo, Egypt, refugee children**
- **New Delhi, India, women**
- **Another woman of power related to Indira Gandhi's daughter in law** *(Sonia Gandhi, wife of Rajiv Gandhi and daughter-in-law of Indira Gandhi occupied Feroze Gandhi's constituency seat again in 2019)*
- **The archer vs a black knight on a black horse** *(The third Horseman carries a pair of balances or weighing scales and rides a black horse and is popularly understood to be Famine indicating the way that bread would have been weighed during a famine. Famine during pandemic? Locusts' attack?)*
- **Flaming lance** *(Missile?)*
- **Christian martyrs** - barbaric torture, where they put people on like a huge rotating wheel *(ISIS making human shields of captives)*

- **Roman commanding general in the Middle Ages**
- **Gaius**
- **Constantinople**
- **August 2017** - black tide? *(Hurricane Harvey?)*
- **Airplanes** *(more troops deployed to Afghanistan; Syria-Lebanon border Raqqa; Boeing 737 crashes)*
- **Pearl Harbor** = Japan
- **Guam** *(threatened by North Korean President Kim Jong Un / August 2017)*
- **Bali, Indonesia**
- **Malawi**
- **South Carolinas** *(hurricanes?)*
- **Epidemic in Europe** *(caution re ISIS? coronavirus?)*
- **Re babies like a scourge, because of all the abortion, weeping mothers**
- **Procession of women with long candles** *(Hong Kong protests?)*
- **Mothers with dead babies** *(mostly children trapped in Raqqa battle - land mines; earthquakes)*
- **Malaria in South Africa** *(South Africa reported just over 9500 indigenous cases of malaria in 2018 – less than half of the 22, 000 cases seen in 2017. To reduce the disease burden, the country has made extra funding from its national treasury available for malaria).*
- **Dengue fever in Thailand** *(The Thailand Department of Disease Control (DDC) issued a national warning over dengue fever this week May 2020)*
- **Insect infestation in Myanmar, Laos, Cambodia**
- *A total of 11 insect pests and their damages inflicted were observed in three tea plantations at weekly intervals during 2012-2013 in Tarpon, Lashio Township, Myanmar. The infestation was high during July associated with heavy rainfall followed by cool conditions, and it was also high in the sites nearer to orchards and crop fields.*

- **Japan** -- are they building a nuclear bomb??? *(easily very capable)*
- **Nuclear bomb technology** *(North Korea, Iran, etc.)*
- **Perfecting science of missile and bomb technology, payback for World War II**
- *(US, missiles, drones, satellites, etc.)*
- **Vietnam** = South Vietnam
- **Duterte** *(extra-judicial killing of Duterte during his anti-drug war campaign numbered tens of thousands)*
- --- end here for now ---

In 2013, I relocated from Massachusetts to Northern Virginia. I felt like a prodigal daughter hungry or rather thirsty for God. I was reeling in from some very painful experiences. In 1998, my mother died from cancer. It was the start of a personal unraveling for me because I had a pretty strong bond with my mother. We were pretty close like we were sisters. Friends come and go, but she had always been my constant best friend. Understandably, when she passed away, I fell into depression which did not get diagnosed until 2001. Despite my clinical depression, I thrived in my career. I climbed up the career ladder and even got into a graduate business management degree program at the country's pioneer business school exclusively for women. I also pursued multiple lines of career in banking, financial services and hospitality throughout the years. I was what they called having a multi-career portfolio. My ultimate career goal was to pursue an executive position in global corporate banking.

I lived in Boston or primarily around Boston, a world class, multi-faceted city of excellence in various engaging pursuits, professional or recreational. It also offered plenty of community activities. It had that feeling of being in a big city but with somehow having the atmosphere of a small town. In 2008, I got married only to get divorced in 2010. The vulnerability from the depression, the stress from the military family life, the immigration issues which permeated the marriage and other countless details made me reflect on my decision to go ahead with the divorce and just move on with my life. Between 2010-2012, I couldn't really focus much at work while trying to rebuild my personal life. The last residence I had in Massachusetts was in the Cape Cod area. After my oldest sister passed away, my brother suggested that I relocate to Virginia. Although I had much hesitation then since I have been used to living independently, I felt like it would be best for me to relocate anyway and start anew.

Faith-wise, I had plenty of religious or Church involvement but since I was a regular volunteer with an official role, it almost felt like it was work. It felt like the richness of a spiritual life was missing. One time, I entered a church, which was on my way home. I purposely attended Mass and took one of the middle pews. So, I was there, right smack almost in the middle of everybody where nobody knew me and no one had to talk to me and vice-versa. I honestly loved it like I had some breathing space and I told God, "Where are you? I am seeking You!" After I have moved to Virginia, the first chance I got to talk to a priest, I told him I was thirsty for God. He said he liked that word, "thirsty."

I wasn't really the religious type then who would be joining parish organizations. I enjoyed life to the fullest in Boston, in the sense that every weekend meant either one among attending friend's parties, checking out new restaurants or checking out new places. A very active social life was my crème de la crème.

In Alexandria, Virginia, I met one of the officers of the Legion of Mary who pursued me relentlessly. Two or three times, I was able to give an excuse that I cannot come. By the third attempt to invite me, the guy knocked at every door in my apartment building to seek me out! I felt guilty enough that he had to go through that just because I intentionally did not give him my apartment number so he would not bother me. Considering that, I agreed to attend the next meeting. To cut the story short, an opportunity opened up where I took charge of the home visitations of Mary's statue to pray rosary with the parish families. I took every opportunity to speak to the parishioners and realized that 9 out of 10 of every person I talked to agreed to a home visit, oftentimes, even very excited welcoming Mary's visit. I also realized that there always seem to be a compelling reason why Mary had to visit a particular home. There were times I had to reschedule the visit and it turned out some other family had a more urgent need to pray. Having become more deeply involved with the Legion of Mary, I was asked to draw a logo for the homeless shelter project. One morning, I had an inclination to attend the 630 AM Mass that day. I usually go to the 8:45 one. After Mass, I thought I would visit the Blessed Sacrament Chapel for a few minutes and pray. As I was praying, I started to doze off. Before I fell asleep, I believe I saw an image of Mary similar to that of Our Lady of Mediatrix or Our Lady of Miraculous Medal, inside the ciborium where the Host is kept.

CHAPTER 7

The Marian Logo

Throughout that day, as I was thinking of how to design the logo, I was trying to figure out how Mary would want it like if it would be the same way I saw her image inside the ciborium. The brass ciborium had a design of sunrays like protruding from the center. That night, as I was drawing the logo, Mary came to my mind's eye where I could perfectly see her beautiful, radiant face, unlike of any human being I ever saw. We started having a very interactive conversation where she was guiding me how to draw the logo. She looked kind of young, maybe around the time she had Jesus, like a young mother, between late teens and early 20's. As I was looking at her face, I felt or thought like, that's probably why she was chosen as Mother of God because it did not seem like there was even a hint of stain in her pure radiance. As I was drawing the logo image, she would instruct me with some details like put more drawing of flowers or extend the sunrays more; color this or that part blue and other detailed stuff. Of course, it crossed my mind that, "wait, these conversations are pretty interactive, Am I just simply imagining things in my mind?" But then, her face radiated with such beauty, purity and simplicity that I thought, I could not just have been imagining this. In addition, our conversations were pretty interactive enough in the sense that when I ask a question, the reply was very immediate without me having to think about it, like in a regular conversation between two people. Also, the fact that our conversation was pretty instructional. She was instructing me how to create the drawing in a very specific way she would like. I learned or read some literature later that she did the same thing in terms of giving specific instructions on how her medals were supposed to be created. Some of the visionaries she spoke to later became saints.

The logo the author drew with direct instructions from Mary during a mystical conversation with her, 2016.

Before our conversation ended after I have drawn the logo, she instructed me to write down some information about four priests in our parish church. As far as I remember, they were very personal information and mostly about relationship with their own fathers. I wrote down the notes just on the first piece of paper that I could grab from what I was working on. I thought later that I perhaps should have kept a copy but I also thought that they were quite personal. I can remember though about something so and so still missing their fathers and how those relationships still pretty much lingered in their hearts and minds. Mary instructed me to give the information I wrote down for the priests. My first thought was, they would think I am crazy! But then nobody can really refuse Mary! I thought that even just with an interactive vision in my mind, if I truly believe in her, then I should do what she says. The next time I attended the Legion of Mary meeting then, I informed the spiritual director about my conversation with Mary. I may have also emailed or informed him ahead of time and I gave plenty of details about how Mary looked like and how I felt during the conversations, like it was pretty much a regular human conversation, except that it's with Mary.

Later on, I found out that the logo I drew had some similarities to Argentina's Our Lady of Lujan. I cannot remember exactly how I figured it out. Maybe I might have seen it on the internet. When I approached the priests with the information I was sent with, I thought that it would just end there! Apparently, that was only the beginning! It has been a very tough, very trying road and there were times I really just wanted to quit talking to Church officials but each time I felt that, I also felt that I am being tugged back in with more and more messages or things to say. I have also developed that relationship with Mary where there's no more questioning involved because the things, she had told me had really come into fruition, so there's really not much room or any room at all for doubt. Not everything could be rosy perfect but I just have to have that trust, although sometimes to me, things don't make much sense. If so, it just means that in due time, she will reveal to me what is meant to be revealed. I seem to understand that better now though.

CHAPTER 8

Meeting Big Boss Daddy

Some things were going on at the parish. One time I attended an event that has something to do with Christ's crown of thorns. I stayed on the grass to watch the parade going on. I saw this guy dressed in a hooded sweatshirt and eyeglasses. I recognized and called him. He said, "Busted. You busted me. The Director of Religious Education wanted me to watch you." He was referring to possibly something going on between myself and my pastor. I just continued on watching the parade. My pastor was on the other side of the crowd. Beaming. I then wrote a letter to the diocese that nothing had been going on between me and the pastor. At least nothing physical. I have told him in the past that I liked him.

One Friday night, I attended the Mass. After the Mass, I approached the pastor. I fondly call him "Papi" because he speaks Spanish. He told me that sometimes it's better just to keep quiet sometimes than talk. I got mad because I thought I did the right thing. I was trying to defend him, defend us. When I got home, I looked for another parish. I was determined to leave. Just as I was looking at another parish, St. Lawrence, Big Boss Daddy showed up in my mind's eye as George Burns. He was eating green apple. He asked me why was I planning to leave. I said, "because I'm mad with Papi." He asked me again. I said

"I'm very mad with Papi." I didn't tell Him that perhaps it would be best if I were just an anonymous parishioner. Something which was actually not bound to happen. Big Boss Daddy told me, "Koochy koochy koo." He was trying to pacify me. I hung in there for a few seconds. After a while, I felt relieved and then said, "Okay, I won't leave then." He just continued munching on His green apple. I asked Him "Why are you eating? Aren't you not supposed to eat anything?" He told me, "I enjoy My creation." I believe He was already halfway through His green apple and then He disappeared. It left me asking "Was I just really talking to God?" I came to understand later that He wanted to be in an understandable form like being in George Burns although He showed Himself later to me as the white bearded guy. I was wondering, "Is that Moses or St. Joseph? Then I exclaimed, "It's Big Boss Daddy!" I have never seen Him before like that. He was in full figure, full view.

There was a time when I heard the priest suggesting on his homily for people to go on confession so I did. I went to one of the four priests that I gave a message of personal revelation to. He suggested that I get therapy. He said the diocese will be happy to pay for my therapy through my pastor and so I did. I went to this place called A&O Clinic. When we arrived, I filled up forms and then waited. I noticed there were plenty of forms talking about their religious and psychiatric services. I joked with my brother who accompanied me and said, "Are they going to make a religious out of me?" with a little bit of a snicker. After a while I got called and talked to my designated therapist. She asked me if I trusted her. I said, "Yes."

When we got home, I kind of felt suspicious. I thought perhaps they were set to determine if I merely had psychiatric issues. I decided to cancel my therapy with A&O and just decided to go back to my already existing therapist whom I put on hold for a while. I spoke with my brother regarding the payment to speak to them. I don't know if he did.

When I met with my therapist, I told him about my experiences and decided to tell him about meeting Big Boss Daddy. I said, "You might think I am crazy but that's what you're here for." He said, "Try me." I said I met Big Boss Daddy. He asked me why I call Him Big Boss Daddy. I said, "I have to do some things for Him so I call Him Big Boss Daddy." He asked me to continue and I just narrated to him things I have been doing. I asked him about his religious orientation. He said that he belonged to a council of men that helps out in the Church. He went inactive for a while but they invited him again so he said yes. He said he belonged to a different tradition than the Catholic. He's a Presbyterian.

I actually liked that he seemed to integrate his religious views into his counseling. He quoted me a saint before for his advice. I told my pastor about it and he explained to me what it meant. I may have just met with him one more time after that and then I decided I don't need counseling anymore.

CHAPTER 9

Visions of Heavenly Personalities

**"Wow, is this interactive? Are they
really interacting with me?"**

"The history of all approved apparitions shows that the Church requires unequivocal evidence of the supernatural. This can be cures, as at Lourdes and Beauraing, or a supernatural prodigy, as at Fatima. The reason from the Church's mystical theology is that most mysticism (as both St. Thomas Aquinas and St. John of the Cross) is mediated by the angels (who have a created angelic nature). What the good angels can do the bad angels can imitate, so that many so-called "supernatural" phenomena are merely preternatural (above human nature, but not above the angelic nature.)

In my experience, and from what I have read, most appearances or apparitions of Mary, did not require the mediation of angels. Mary can, and pretty much can choose and have chosen how she would appear to her visionaries. It also seems to be a pattern in some cases that she has given distinct personal revelations that people can confirm as true and significant. I did have visions of angels. They look like very powerful beings. The body looks like human, and I believe that the garb is almost the same as the one

41

we would see with St. Michael the archangel. My intuition tells me, that angels do have classification of function or work, but the guardian angels are kind of the same St. Michael type. Seeing an angel would be such an immensely overwhelming experience that would make one stricken with awe, mysterious wonder and fascination. From what I saw in my vision, an angel's wings about two feet from about the shoulders to the tip of the edge of the wings. The wing span is probably about five feet from each side, so when it's all stretched out, imagine, like about 8 to 10 feet of glowing, very pure, kind of feathery white! It's quite unlike the bird feathers but it has that very light almost feathery texture. With that pure white glow, I believe it kept me from seeing much of the details of the wings but I do recall that it's voluminous enough that when an angel appears and wraps its wings around you, you would be totally wrapped in such a majestic might for protection. This made me think about those circumstances where people get to be in accidents yet miraculously survive.

In my visions, I also saw St. Michael the Archangel several times that I have called him like "my hero best friend" because I believe the first time, he appeared to me, he was busy fighting demons. He had like a lance. He was pretty much dressed the same way in his representations. After the fighting, he had a brief moment and a chance to look towards me and he smiled. I thought, "My hero! My real-life action hero!" He's actually pretty good looking but not in human terms. He radiates with such confidence. It's more like an inner glow. The term I used was "heavenly personalities" because I have met plenty of them in my visions. The beauty or handsomeness is not in the physicality because they no longer have physical bodies but it is like this glow of radiance which emanates from them. One time, in my earlier visions, new to being a mystic, I have also met St. Joseph, Jesus' foster father and St. Jude. I got confused because they were almost wearing the same attire. One of them was wearing an orange and a green garb. I saw them walking by heading somewhere. They both looked at me and smiled as if to greet me and my reaction was, "Wow, is this interactive? They're really interacting with me?" I have also met in one of my visions, Joseph, from the Biblical story, known for his coat and later on interpreted dreams. We talked about his coat because that's the way I recognized him. He said that it wasn't really that fancy or technicolor, but at that time, clothing was more like sack clothes so color already makes it fancy. From the people from this century, it was St. Pope John XXIII. I had a mystical conversation with. He seemed very pleasant and very grandfatherly. I had a vision about a boat. I didn't know then that a boat is like a symbolism for the Church. I asked him if he wanted me to say anything in his behalf, referring to the vision of the boat. He said, "They'll understand." The first time I saw St. Pope John Paul II in my visions, he was making this gesture of like looking through a telescope with his hands. I remembered he always made those gestures either before getting off or getting inside the plane. He said to me that it is like a very joyful occasion looking at those crowds of people awaiting him. It's like his goofy way to express his joy! All these are pretty interesting! I should really be writing a book about my mystical visions!

There was a time when I received a brief vision about Pope Francis with his cheek and clothes bloodied and I told my contact priests about this. A few days after, news arrived that Pope Francis had an accident inside the bus. He had blood on his cheeks coming from the head bump.

CHAPTER 10

Visions of After-Life

I wanted to double-check the Vatican version of Our Lady's messages at Fatima to make sure that I am not missing anything. I read a title which said "Visions of Hell." I did not want to read the document as I did not want to be influenced by it as I present my own visions of hell, purgatory and of heaven, all in connection with my conversations with Mary.

During one of my prayer sessions during that 54-day Rosary Novena, Mary showed me a vision of hell and purgatory. At another session, I was shown what I believe was a vision of Heaven. During these times, I prayed the rosary accompanied by or using the Gregorian chant. The holy music is kind of like a protective barrier for our sacred conversations from whatever may be lingering with malice or contradictory intentions. The holy music also brings me into quite a highly focused state which makes it easier for me to look at the details in my visions. Other music such as Litany of the Saints, also the Gregorian chant brings me into that ecstatic state. There were times I would play the music over and over because it's just like I couldn't get enough of that highly altered state of ecstasy. It's kind of like a drug, really.

During that 54-day Novena period, Mary did not really forewarn me of what she wanted to show me during that night.

One time, while praying the Gregorian chant, Mary showed me visions of hell and purgatory.

I was talking with Mary in my vision. We were like in a platform stage actually. Then I saw God the Father and Jesus. The Father actually reminded me of King Neptune in the movies that I saw. He had a very kingly bearing. I couldn't remember His face exactly because the white hair and the white beard was more highlighted. He has a physical built that is really very commanding. I can't accurately capture with words just that His presence is VERY COMMANDING, VERY POWERFUL, VERY KINGLY. Jesus was there, too. Both were wearing like white tunics? Something like what Jesus wore then. So, I had to wait for an angel to accompany me for my visit. An angel with huge white wings on a white horse came and the Father pointed with His left hand, instructing the angel like a "go-ahead" signal to accompany me.

The first place I visited was supposed to be hell. The place was very dark. There were dark, dark, frightening clouds above. The place was very dark, very gloomy except for some fire embers here and there like what you see in the movies after a village had been ransacked and burnt.

What was more frightening was the state of the souls of the people there. I saw souls of people walking around like in a constant worry. They were like heavily burdened with all those negative emotions of anxiety, of constant worry, of like terror, of anguish. For a few moments, I felt what they felt and it was very suffocating that I couldn't breathe. Physically, I started crying from when I was seeing in my visions. I was suffocating and maybe feeling like gasping for air. The only time I was able to breathe was when I saw Jesus coming towards me. He was actually picking me up from that place and then I believe motioned me or the angel to accompany me to the next place I was supposed to visit. The angel protected me while I was there. The angel was pretty authoritative to the demons or spoke with authority and told them to stay away from me. I thought that the demons looked red like that of rage or fury. The difference with living people though is that those alive are capable of several emotions. In that hell, it seemed like that they were just stuck.

When I saw Jesus coming towards me, it came to my mind that Jesus is the only one allowed to go there without being affected by that surroundings. He's the relief. It's kind of like He cannot be soiled with that environment. I felt happy again when I saw Him because I felt relieved that I could breathe again! After that I was with the angel again and we visited Purgatory. In Purgatory, it was still a dimly lit place but without those terrible, negative emotions. The souls I saw were like peeking downward through a circular hole and they could see some people down there, and they can also hear some music. I thought that if I get to see or visit heaven next, I may just want to stay there! Soon enough, the angel and myself went back to see Mary, the Father and Jesus who seemed like waiting to see me, after my visit. I prostrated myself in front of the Father and Jesus. I was left with Mary to talk some more. She told me that she appreciated my gesture towards the Father and Jesus. I believe I told her that I was pretty happy that I was able to breathe again after I saw Jesus!

The more interesting one was my vision of Heaven. Remember when Jesus said, "there are many rooms in my Father's place." In my vision, I was like in a huge, huge room like a grand hall. The hall of famer Saints as I call them, because these are the most popular ones with the biggest names as most requested for prayers were supposed to gather for the dance. They were dressed like in a palatial regalia. It was pretty much like having a ball at the Palace. I thought though that I wanted to go explore and check out other rooms then, so I left the ball and I saw other huge rooms. In another one, there was a huge number of people but the people looked very ordinary, more like in peasant clothes but they were also very happy, very joyful. They were dancing with the music and they saw me and invited me to join them, so I did for a little bit until I woke myself up from the vision. I thought that those people are saints with a smaller "s."

After writing down my visions and reading the Vatican document about the messages in Fatima, it just reinforces my intuitive thoughts that I need to see the whole, bigger picture and confidently rely on the mystical guidance provided to me.

CHAPTER 11

The 54-Day Rosary

Mama had a musical jewelry musical box. She always expressed she wanted one and that she was looking for it. It might have been a gift to her from one of my siblings when they found the type she was looking for. When the top of the musical box is opened, it plays a tune and the little ballerina would dance. I think the tune was "The Swan Lake." Interestingly, during my first week I arrived in Boston, Mama and I took the "Swan Boat" ride at the Boston Common.

I still have to think about the full meaning of the musical box but early on, after my initial vision of Mary, I have started praying the rosary sung in Gregorian chant on rather a nightly basis. She also asked me or instructed me to pray and accompany the Church for the 54-day rosary prayer novena that was being held at that time. It was supposed to end on October 7, 2016. Aside from my prayers, my sacrifice will be to see whatever revelations she will show me. Most of the time, at that time, it had been related to the almost nauseating visions of almost every conceivable evil that humanity had been capable of. I did not write it beforehand but those visions were about the inhumane events that happened within that 100 years before the Fatima Centennial, but it focused mostly on the horrors of the world war. I was like inside the movie frame, where I see actually what was taking place but I was only an invisible part of the scene.

The scenes I saw were horrific. Some of them were about men, women and children running frantically to hide from the Nazi soldiers. They had basements in their houses where these people hid and they were holding off breaths in fear of being caught by the soldiers. Some were just the people on the streets during the same scene also frantically running to seek somewhere to hide before the soldiers arrive. Some visions were about the soldiers in foxholes. I saw some of the bloodied bodies of dead soldiers with flies hovering around it. Some soldiers were still alive, hiding in the foxholes getting their machine guns ready and there were bombs exploding around them. At another vision, the most dreadful one was like a prisoner camp set in fire and I can see the people frantic, yelling and screaming, getting scorched from the fire but they were pretty helpless inside that burning structure.

These visions did not happen during one seating or one prayer session. It was a couple of prayer sessions which almost made me afraid or uncomfortable of what I might see but Mary was there with me. So, in almost of all these scenes, it seemed like I was right there at the scene that I could see the details, smell, hear the sounds and feel my own physical reaction to the scenes. There were times, I felt like throwing up because the scenes were just so nauseating and I told Mary that but she asked me to keep looking explaining to me that there's a reason why she's showing all these to me. "Keep looking. There's a purpose why I am showing this to you," which I interpreted as to truly comprehend in my heart what happened within that 100 years of Fatima and the Pope Leo XIII prophecy. These horrors should not happen again. The Fatima Centennial was supposed to be celebrated the next year, 2017.

At another instance, Mary showed me something about the persecutions of Christians by the brutal ISIS. There was a man on his knees with his hands tied behind his back. A brutal man cracked his head with a large rock. I saw the man's soul like halfway leaving his body and Mary stood beside him comforting him. I saw the man smile as he recognized Mary.

My visions had a semblance of the vision that Pope Leo XIII had when the events of the 20th century were revealed to him by the Lord on October 13, 1884. He saw wars, immorality, genocide and apostasy on a large scale. Pope Leo XIII was even reported to have turned pale and collapsed like dead. The people standing nearby and rushed to his side found him alive but looked frightened. Immediately following the disturbing vision, he sat down and wrote the prayer to St. Michael.

In my insightful and inspired interpretation of the Marian prophecies, what is also very significant to note is that how details connect together and the consistency of a theme expressed in the messages. The connections bind and reinforce the points to create a larger picture for a clearer understanding. Apparitions, cannot necessarily be interpreted as a stand-alone message, there is a deeper, fuller story woven with them. Time needs to be understood in God's context, where everything happening is at the present. Time does not necessarily have to be understood as a linear progression. There's something co-terminus or contemporaneous about the Marian prophecies. It's like everything occurring at the present, thus, there are details that connect and are themed with each other. This is one of the differences that I offer my insights into the Marian prophecies. The other points are related to my mystical visions and life experiences with the people around me but particularly with Mama and St. Pope John Paul II.

CHAPTER 12

Lectio Divina

Intrigued by my experiences, I visited the Blessed Sacrament often because I knew that's where I can find God. I have also started an electronic media relationship with the people in the Church studying me. One time I got offended because I read the word "frankincense." I thought it to meant "Frankenstein" and "incense." I went to Church and I cried after the Mass. My pastor saw me crying. I ran to the Blessed Sacrament to tell Big Boss Daddy that I was probably unfit for the job. There was a Bible at the shelves by the front door. I felt like God was telling me to pick it up and read. I picked up the Bible and opened it up. I found the Book of Judith.

I read the Book of Judith and the story where God told her to tell the religious leaders of her time that they were wrong. She was the smallest of them all, she was just a widow, a nobody but God equipped her with things to say to the religious leaders.

I decided to return to the electronic messaging and wrote them some more stuff for them to notice me. Almost in a very taunting way. I started writing more just as how I am inspired.

At first, I didn't know or I was not sure how to call myself. I didn't know which saint to follow. The idea of St. Hildegard von

Bingen was floated around. She was an unruly mystic. Kind of like me. She had a problematic relationship with her superior.

It was at that time that I was also introduced more to the music of YouTube. I actually learned about YouTube from my ex-husband. We would play songs to each other. He liked the R Kelly songs. I found some more songs that I liked.

One of my earliest writings was about: "There's something (human) about Mary. At this time, my friends from the Legion of Mary have started calling me Mary. It had reference to the Biblical scene where Jesus was on the Cross and He introduced John and Mary to each other. It had reference to me and my pastor meeting each other. I took on the name "Mary" as a pen name. Later on, I added his last name as I was inspired to do so. I called myself "Mary Z."

CHAPTER 13

Some Writings

Out of reflections, I wrote a few articles.

<u>**From the blog Mary Z Rewriting the Faith**</u>

"There's Something (Human) About Mary."

People have given me the nickname of Mary. My inspiration that comes from the Lord is that people have forgotten or refuses to acknowledge that God is the Creator. Throughout human history, the single most offensive act against God is refusing to acknowledge that He is "I AM." That He is God the Creator. A prophet in the Old Testament lamented in His behalf, that it seems like the pot went to the Potter and said, "you did not create me." Similarly, it was the pride of Lucifer, thinking that his beauty equated him to God caused his downfall.

My inspiration is my conversations with God through my mental visions. God delights so much in His creations. We are indeed made in His image and likeness, such that we can see the delight of a human father with his children, if his heart is in the right place.

I also think that God is reminding us how He had created us to be beautiful creatures supposed to delight in our humanity, and not perverted against His intention.

God has blessed me so many kinds of talents for His own purpose. One of those talents is a creative love for music. I wanted to share this with you, hoping it will also inspire you in celebrating our common humanity, made in the image and likeness of our Creator. Amen.

> *"This Girl is on Fire" by Alicia Keyes*
> *"I Believe I can Fly" by R Kelly*
> *"Proud Mary" by Tina Turner*
> *"I'd Like to Teach the World to Sing" (Coca-cola commercial)*
> *"Thank You for the Music" by Amanda Seyfried*
> *"Here I Am Lord"*
> *"I Am Alive" by Celine Dion*
> *"A Change is Gonna Come" by Sam Cooke and Brian Owens*
> *"Love Never Felt So Good" by Michael Jackson*

From the blog Mary Z Rewriting the Faith

The Forgotten Apocalyptic Visions of the Prophet Isaiah

I prayed to Big Boss Daddy and pretty much just started to take note of verses that spoke to me. This was probably around 2016 or early 2017.

> **Isaiah 29:16** *"They turn everything upside down. Which is more important, the potter or the clay? Can something a man has made tell him, "You*

didn't make me"? Or can it say to him, "You don't know what you're doing?[2]

Isaiah 24:1-5 *"The Lord is going to devastate the earth and leave it desolate. He will twist the earth's surface and scatter its people. The earth will lie shattered and ruined. The Lord has spoken and it will be done. The earth dries up and withers, the whole world grows weak; both earth and sky decay. The people have defiled the earth by breaking God's laws and by violating the covenant he made to last forever."*[3]

Isaiah 24: 6-10 *"So God has pronounced a curse on the earth. Its people are paying for what they have done. Fewer and fewer remain alive. The grapevines wither, and wine is becoming scarce. Everyone who was once happy is now sad and drums has ceased. There is no more happy singing over wine; no one enjoys its taste anymore. In the city, everything is in chaos and people lock themselves in their houses for safety."*[4]

In the year 2020, there have been several chaotic protests over the killing of a black man, George Floyd. A policeman knelt with his knee over Floyd's neck for 8 minutes and 46 seconds.

The protests started in Minneapolis on May 26, 2020. It was the day after George Floyd, an African-American man was killed during a police arrest. On June 6, there were an estimated half a million people who joined the protests in 550 places across the country. Protests continued through the weekend of June 19. It

---

[2] Good News Bible. American Bible Society, New York. 1976. p. 770

[3] Ibid., p. 764.

[4] Ibid., p. 764.

overlapped with bringing awareness to observations of Juneteenth. As of July 3, protests had continued to swarm throughout the entire month of June in many cities, with protests occurring in over 40% of the counties in the United States. According to poll estimates, between 15 and 26 million people participated in the United States, making the protests potentially the largest movement in terms of participation in US history.

The protests spread to over 2,000 cities and towns in all 50 states and all five permanently-inhabited territories, as well as in over 60 other countries. The demonstrators support those seeking justice and the wider Black Lives Matter movement, and speaking out against police brutality. Continuous protests had been seen in many cities since Floyd's killing, such as in New York with 21 consecutive days of protests as of June 17, 2020. Many protests were accompanied by violence with some large cities seeing large scale rioting, looting and burning of businesses and police cars. There were also many instances of police brutality. The wave of protests and unrest were likened to the long, hot summer of 1967 and the King assassination riots, both of which saw riots in over a hundred cities across the United States.[5]

Outside the United States, protests against the killing of George Floyd, racism and police brutality also occurred, notably in the cities of Auckland, Barcelona, Berlin, Brisbane, Madrid, Melbourne, Copenhagen, Dublin, Accra, Lagos, Nairobi, Cape Town, Paris, Perth, Rio de Janeiro, Sydney, Tel Aviv, Seoul, Tokyo, Vienna and Athens as well as in the countries of Canada and the United Kingdom. Protests have occurred in over 60 countries and on all continents except Antarctica.[6]

With regards to people locking themselves down for safety, due to the covid-19 pandemic, curfews, quarantines and similar

---

[5] List of George Floyd protests in the United States. Retrieved March 25, 2021 from https://en.wikipedia.org/wiki/List_of_George_Floyd_protests_in_the_United_States.

[6] Ibid.

restrictions (variously described as stay-at-home orders, shelter-in-place orders, *cordons sanitaires*, shutdowns or lockdowns) have been implemented in numerous countries and territories around the world. These lockdowns were established to prevent the further spread of the severe acute respiratory syndrome coronavirus 2 (SARS-CoV-2), which causes COVID-19. By April 2020, about half of the world's population was under lockdown. More than 3.9 billion people in more than 90 countries or territories have been asked or ordered to stay at home by their governments.

Second and third wave of lockdowns, mostly in Europe, have also occurred.[7]

> **Isaiah 27:9**: *"But Israel's sins will be forgiven only when the stones of pagan altars are ground up like chalk, and no more symbols of the goddess Asherah or incense altars are left."*[8]

> **Isaiah 26: 20-21**: *"Go, into your houses, my people and shut the door behind you. Hide yourselves for a little while until God's anger is over."*[9]

Blindness and Perversity

> **Isaiah 29: 9-10** *"Go ahead and be stupid! Go ahead and be blind! Get drunk without any wine! Stagger without drinking a drop! The Lord has made you drowsy, ready to fall into a deep sleep. The prophets*

---

[7] "Covid-19 Lockdowns" Retrieved from https://en.wikipedia.org/wiki/COVID-19_lockdowns, March 25, 2021.

[8] Good News Bible. American Bible Society, New York. 1976. P. 777.

[9] Ibid., p. 777.

should be the eyes of the people, but God has blindfolded them."[10]

Personally, I think too many times people who read into the signs of the times, quickly resort to the Book of Revelations. I believe though there is a sacred reason I have come across these apocalyptic visions of Isaiah. I honestly think this is what is being fulfilled now. And the prophecy of Pope Benedict XVI shall come to pass.

> **Isaiah 29: 11-12** *"The meaning of every prophetic vision will be hidden from you. It will be like a sealed scroll. If you take it to someone who knows how to read and ask him to read it to you, he will say he can't because it is sealed. If you give it to someone who can't read and ask him to read it to you, he will answer that he doesn't know how."[11]*

> **Isaiah 29: 13-16** *"The Lord said, "These people claim to worship me, but their words are meaningless, and their hearts are somewhere else. Their religion is nothing but human rules and traditions, which they have simply memorized. So, I will startle them one unexpected blow after another. Those who are wise will turn out to be fools, and all their cleverness will be useless. They turn everything upside down. Which is more important, the potter or the clay? Can something a man has made tell him, "You didn't make me"? Or can it say to him, "You don't know what you're doing?[12]*

---

[10] Ibid., p. 777

[11] Ibid., p. 770.

[12] Ibid., p. 769.

The Revelation of Knowledge: Priest and Prophet

> **Isaiah 28: 7-10** *"Even the prophets and the priests are so drunk that they stagger. They have drunk so much wine and liquor that they stumble in confusion. The prophets are too drunk to understand the visions that God sends, and the priests are too drunk to decide the cases that are brought to them. The tables where they sit are all covered with vomit, and not a clean spot is left. They complain about me. They say, "who does that man think he's teaching? Who needs is message? It's only good for babies that have just stopped nursing! He is trying to teach us letter by letter, line by line, lesson by lesson."[13]*

God and Pope Speaks of Remnant People

> **Isaiah 26: 5** *"He has humbled those who were proud; he destroyed the strong city they lived in, and sent its walls crushing into the dust."[14]*

Cardinal Joseph Ratzinger, who later became Pope Benedict XVI, wrote, "The Church will become small." He claims that "the church will become small and will have to start afresh more or less from the beginning."

In Pope Benedict XVI's own words, "she will no longer be able to inhabit many of the edifices she built in prosperity. As the number of her adherents diminishes....she will lose many of her social privileges...As a small society, (the Church) will make much bigger demands on the initiative of her individual members.

---

[13] Ibid., p. 768.
[14] Ibid., p. 766.

It will be hard-going for the Church, for the process of crystallization and clarification will cost her much valuable energy. It will make her poor and cause her to become the Church of the meek...The process will be long and wearisome as was the road from the false progressivism on the eve of the French Revolution --- when a bishop might be thought smart if he made fun of dogmas and even insinuated that the existence of God was by no means certain...But when the trial of this sifting is past, a great power will flow from a more spiritualized and simplified Church. Men in a totally planned world will find themselves unspeakably lonely. If they have completely lost sight of God, they will feel the whole horror of their poverty. Then they will discover the little flock of believers as something wholly new. They will discover it as a hope that is meant for them, an answer for which they have always been searching in secret.

And so, it seems certain to me that the Church is facing very hard times. The real crisis has scarcely begun. We will have to count on terrific upheavals. But I am equally certain about what will remain at the end: not the Church of the political cult, which is dead already, but the Church of faith. She may well no longer be the dominant social power to the extent that she was until recently; but she will enjoy a fresh blossoming and be seen as man's home, where he will find life and hope beyond death."

This is a prophetic article written by Cardinal Joseph Ratzinger: "The Church will become small." It was republished in Catholic Education.org from "Faith and the Future" (San Francisco: Ignatius Press, 2009). The original publication of Faith and Future was 1969.)

Redemption: "They shall keep My name Holy."

Isaiah 30: 18-21. *"And yet the Lord is waiting to be merciful to you. He is ready to take pity on you because he always does what is right. Happy are* *those who put their trust in the Lord. You people who live in Jerusalem will not weep anymore. The Lord is compassionate and when you cry to him for help, he will answer you. The Lord will make you go through hard times, but he himself will be there to teach you, and you will not have to search him for him anymore. If you wander off the road to the right or the left, you will hear his voice behind you saying, 'Here is the road. Follow it."* [15]

Isaiah 29: 22-24. *"So now the Lord, the God of Israel, who rescued Abraham from trouble, says, "My people, you will not be disgraced any longer, and your faces will no longer be pale with shame. When you see the children that I will give you, then you will acknowledge that I am the holy God of Israel. You will honor me and stand in awe of me. Foolish people will learn to understand and those who are always grumbling will be glad to be taught"* [16]

Isaiah 30:8 *"God told me to write down in a book what the people are like, so that there would be a permanent record of how evil they are."* [17]

Isaiah 25:9 *"When it happens, everyone will say, "He is our God! We have put our trust in him, and he has rescued us. He is the Lord! We have put our trust in him, and now we are happy and joyful because he has saved us."* [18]

---

[15] Ibid., p. 771.

[16] Ibid., p. 770.

[17] Ibid., p. 770.

[18] Ibid., p. 766

CHAPTER 14

The La Salette Prophecies

"Rome will lose the Faith and become the seat of the Antichrist."

"... the abomination will be seen in the holy places; in the convents the flowers of the Church will putrefy, and the devil will establish himself as king of all hearts. Let those who are at the head of religious communities be on their guard concerning the persons they are to receive, because the devil will use all his malice to introduce into religious orders persons given to sin, for disorders and love of carnal pleasures will be widespread over the whole earth.[19]

La Salette, 1846

At that time when the electronic communication had started between me and those verifying my being a mystic and its purpose, the usual method of verifying authenticity was quite rigorous. It was a very unnerving process designed to yielding. I pretty much talked to Mary about that, unloading my complaints. She said she completely understands what's in my heart. It felt like

---

[19] "The Pope in Red," Retrieved from http://www.thepopeinred.com/secret.htm. March 26, 2021.

a mentor speaking. There's that sense that I can feel what's in her heart and she can feel what's in mine. Sort of to help me out with what I needed, she asked me to keep quiet for a period of time, and not say anything back. That was supposed to be a practice and discipline to my will and have a much stronger resolve, both head and heart, for what I have to do. It was also supposed to be a discipline for patience, especially at that time when my temper was much, much shorter arising from life circumstances.

Mary usually gives a specific period of time, pretty much like in her other personal revelations. During that time, I agreed to be quiet and not to talk back, I believe the Church authorities may have misinterpreted it as reinforcing their presuppositions and they heightened their irritations much more. Agreeing with Mary about the silence, I would just pray and feel the stress and my skin was just breaking out. Usually, the marks were on my face and on my arms. There was a time I combined baby oil and holy water from Our Lady of Lourdes to help ease the rashes and the marks. There was one time I was praying to God, and I could just feel like the Father's anger. What I did was I would hold my arm to keep Him from taking action. I could not speak at that time, so I would just put on the clock on my phone and an image of the calculator to express that, hey look, *there's time and there's a calculator.* There will be recompense for this but I couldn't say those things directly.

Last year, there were series of super hurricanes that really felt like an unleash of anger. However, it all makes sense to me now, as all of that was also in the message of the La Salette.

What really stunned me when I read the La Salette prophecy was the mention about the year 2000. It refers to that year with a significance. It stunned me because I thought then that nobody would really believe what Mama told me, so I just kept mum about it. Kind of like a little secret. Back to when I was a kid, Mama pointed out to me Jesus' hands with His Sacred Heart statue. One hand was pointing to His heart and then the other hand was giving a blessing with two upright fingers. She meant that the two upright fingers were referring to the year 2000 when Christ the Savior will be coming back. I don't know if she got the story from our elders who seemed to have like fascinating stories but at the same time, offers pretty simple but plausible explanation of things. Mama told me one time about one of our ancestors, one of our elders, who probably recovered from a coma. When she woke up, she recalled about being to a place where there were candles. An old man greeted her and found that her candle was still burning meaning it wasn't her time yet to leave the world so she had to come back. She recovered from the coma. There were other stories, really amazing and almost unbelievable but I believed her because I thought sometimes elders have a different perception and expression of truth. They're like the native people who are very much keen to the natural world, their knowledge is sophisticated in a very different way.

I was stunned to read about the mention of the year 2000 in the secret message of La Salette. Mary's messages often remain as secrets until the designated time they could be revealed as per Mary's instructions. It was the same thing with Sr. Lucia of Fatima. The Lady instructed her not to reveal the message until after a specific period of time.

The children of La Salette adamantly refused to reveal the "secret" messages, until, in 1851, they were convinced to write the secrets and send them to the Pope for his eyes only. Maximin wrote his secret in July, but several weeks later, at the behest of his friend M. Dausse, he wrote a prophetic fantasy which Dausse took to be authentic. Maximin often took this approach to those who would pester him with requests for prophecies, and he insisted that the "secret" given to Dausse was such a fiction.[20]

My presumption or interpretation of the situation here is that it is **quite a daunting responsibility be able to foretell or to harbor knowledge of events or occurrences that would significantly**

---

[20] Retrieved from "The Pope in Red," http://www.thepopeinred.com/secret.htm. March 26, 2021.

impact time, populations or generations of people. I would totally understand if the children learned that early enough with all the potential ridicule or pestering skepticism with how people could or would react and Mary has been sensitively protective enough of her visionaries by designating a specific time as to when such matters could be revealed.

I had a vision of Mary as Our Lady of La Salette at the same time an earthquake occurred in a town in Italy. I was just finishing taking a shower when Mary showed up in my vision. I wrote in my journal:

"That night of the earthquake in Italy, I woke up around 12:30 AM but I did not feel like doing the rosary immediately. I had a snack and took a shower. While I was almost done with the shower, the Blessed Mother came into my visions and said, "Post the images of the La Salette." By the time I was able to pray the rosary, it was already around 1:30 AM EST. It usually takes me an hour to go through the Gregorian chanted rosary prayers. After I finished it, I started posting the images of Our Lady of La Salette and I myself went through familiarizing myself with it. I also posted some pictures of animals yawning like they were getting ready to go to sleep. I did not realize until I heard the news that by the time I was posting the crying images of Our Lady of La Salette, an earthquake was about to hit Italy. It was around 2:30 or 3:30 AM EST. News report confirmed that an earthquake of 6.2 magnitude hit Central Italy occurred 3:36 CEST local time on August 24, 2016. There were 295 deaths, 400 injured and 4,000 made homeless. The epicenter was close to Accumoli, with its hypocenter approximately 47 miles (75 km) southeast of Perugia and 28 miles (45 km) north of L'Aquila. The borders near the area were that of Umbria, Lazio, Abruzzo and Marche regions.[21]

---

[21] "Italy Earthquake 2016" Geographical Association. Retrieved from https://www.geography.org.uk/teaching-resources/earthquakes-tsunamis/italy-2016. March 26, 2021.

It was further reported that the towns and villages in the Umbria, Lazo and Marche regions suffered the most damage. They include Amatrice, Accumoli, Reuters, Posta and Pescara del Tronto. Another 4.8 magnitude earthquake followed at 6:28 AM local time on August 26 which caused more damage to crumbled buildings and hampering rescue efforts further. This was one of the over 500 aftershocks recorded by the officials since the initial quake.[22]

In Amatrice, almost the entire historic town was destroyed, despite many buildings being reinforced since they were built in the 16th, 17th and 18th centuries. The village of Pescara del Tronto was levelled to the ground.[23]

It was determined by the US Geological Survey (USGS) that the earthquake was caused by shallow normal faulting in the Central Apennines, where the Eurasia plate moves towards the northeast with respect with Africa (at an average rate of 24 mm a year.) Normal faulting happens when plates are torn apart and a sudden release in tension causes one of the plates to drop.[24]

Mary's messages at La Salette started a string of apparitions with a particular message about Christ's Church vis-à-vis world events and of what is to be averted, what the Church will experience and what should happen. In the Bible's New Testament, there were two major events were Mary spoke, the first one with the Annunciation where she proclaimed Magnificat! And the second one was when she prompted Jesus to perform His first miracle during the wedding at Cana. Throughout the life events of Jesus, there was no mention of anything about what Mary had said, even throughout the Lord's Passion, Death and Resurrection. Yet, after her assumption to heaven, she had appeared in apparitions all over the place. Even the contemporary National Geographic magazine

---

[22] Ibid.
[23] Ibid.
[24] Ibid.

had an article on Mary as the most powerful woman throughout history. Much had been written about her apparitions. Most of what the Catholic Church had declared as official and miraculous apparitions ended up with building a Church at the site where she had appeared.

Another Famine?

In her apparition at La Salette, Mary spoke of a famine. "A great famine will come. Before the famine comes, children under the age of seven will begin to tremble and will die in the arms of those who hold them. The others will do penance through hunger. The nuts will go bad, the grapes will become rotten." It kind happened all over again in 2020. Not that there was lack of food but millions of people lost their jobs and became food insecure. Unemployed people in several states lined up for food and children were infected with a rare disease and died.

"Come near, my children, be not afraid; I am here to tell you great news. If my people will not submit, I shall be forced to let fall the arm of my Son. It is so strong, so heavy, that I can no longer withhold it. For how long do I suffer for you! If I would not have my Son abandon you, I am compelled to pray to him without ceasing; And as to you, you take not heed of it. However, much you pray, however, much you do, you will never recompense the pains I have taken for you.

If the harvest is spoilt, it is all on your account. I gave you warning last year with the potatoes (pommes de terre) but you did not heed it. On the contrary, when you found the potatoes spoilt, you swore, you took the name of my Son in vain. They will continue to decay, so that by Christmas, there will be none left.

The French term "pommes de terre" puzzled Melanie, since in Patois, the word for potatoes was "truffas" where pommes meant apple exclusively.

The Lady repeated her previous statement in Patois and continued in the same dialect.

"If you have wheat, it is no good to sow it; all you sow the insects will eat and what comes up will fall into dust when you thresh it. There will come a great famine. Before the famine comes, the children under seven years of age will be seized with trembling and will die in the hands of those who hold them; the others will do penance by famine. The walnuts will become bad and the grapes will rot."[25]

A significant point in the La Salette prophecy was about the famine which was brought about by a new strain in the potatoes. I brought this to the attention of the people trying to verify my authenticity.

The presumed Church people reacted to me rather sarcastically. They had potatoes distributed via the Church's food ministry. My jaw dropped. I read something in a farmers' manual that potatoes tend to increase the capability of wireless technology.

In the meantime, the immense gross food insecurity did occur. In other words, "a famine" did occur.

In the US alone, Feeding America projected that 45 million people and 15 million children went food insecure in 2020.[26] In 2021, the projection was lower. It was 42 million people (1 in 8) and 13 million children (1 in 6). In 2017, according to The Nation, there was about 40 million who were food insecure. [27] There were

---

[25] "The Pope in Red," Retrieved from http://www.thepopeinred.com/secret.htm. March 26, 2021.

[26] "The Impact of Coronavirus in Food Insecurity in 2020 and 2021" Feeding America.Org. Retrieved from https://www.feedingamerica.org/sites/default/files/2021-03/National%20Projections%20Brief_3.9.2021_0.pdf. March 26, 2021.

[27] Ibid.

five more million people in 2021 than in 2017. With much help, the expectation was lowered for 2021.

2020 was also the year that food insecurity was in focus because as of April 2020, 20.6 million people had lost their jobs. The unemployment rate was at 14.7%, a level unseen since the Great Depression in the 1930's. In the 2007-2009 Great Recession, only 8.7 million Americans lost jobs. Before the pandemic, the United States noted a 50-year unemployment low in with just 3.5% of Americans unemployed. According to USA Today, 18 million are expected to be temporary when the pandemic recedes.[28]

I also brought to their attention the possibility of a new viral strain. At that time, the medications for HIV were at its last combination. If the strain mutates, there will not be much hope for humanity. Gay, lesbians, bisexual and transgendered people tend to abound too.

Center for Disease Control estimates indicate that about 20% of the US population or approximately one in every five people in the U.S. had a sexually transmitted infection on any given day in 2018. It is costing the American healthcare system nearly $16 billion in healthcare costs alone.

But the new viral strain was actually found in SARS CoV-2. It stands for severe acute respiratory syndrome coronavirus 2. This virus causes the COVID-19 disease.[29] SARS-CoV2 is a coronavirus, belonging to a large group of RNA viruses. They are named "corona" because their membranes are studded by spike-like proteins. They have been known to be infectious for decades but were initially recognized for only mild illnesses

---

[28] US job losses due to COVID-19 highest since Great Depression. University of Minnesota Center for Infectious Disease Research and Policy. Retrieved from https://www.cidrap.umn.edu/news-perspective/2020/05/us-job-losses-due-covid-19-highest-great-depression. March 26, 2021.

[29] "What is SARS CoV-2?" Webmd.com. Retrieved from https://www.webmd.com/lung/qa/what-is-sarscov2 March 27, 2021.

such as the common cold but now they are newly capable of infecting humans to causes a disease named COVID-19. The initial COVID-19 cases were identified in Wuhan, China in the late 2019. It has since spread to other areas of China and around the globe.[30]

The most profound thought in the La Salette prophecy is its implications to the religious people:

"The priests, ministers of my Son, the priests, by their wicked lives, by their irreverence and their impiety in the celebration of the holy mysteries, by their love of money, their love of honors and pleasures, and the priests have become cesspools of impurity. Yes, the priests are asking vengeance, and vengeance is hanging over their heads. Woe to the priests and to those dedicated to God who by their unfaithfulness and their wicked lives are crucifying my Son again! The sins of those dedicated to God cry out towards Heaven and call for vengeance, and now vengeance is at their door, for there is no one left to beg mercy and forgiveness for the people. There are no more generous souls; there is no one left worthy of offering a stainless sacrifice to the Eternal for the sake of the world."

"God will strike in an unprecedented way.[31]"

USA Today reported that as of November 11, 2019, *Bishop Accountability,* a website that tracks accusations has named 6,433 priests, brothers and Catholic school officials accused of abuse. Additionally, 154 archdioceses and dioceses have released the names of 4,771 credibly accused clerics, according to Jeff Anderson

---

[30] "What is coronavirus and how do we develop new treatments" The Jackson Laboratory. Retrieved from https://www.jax.org/coronavirus#. March 27, 2021.

[31] "Apparition of the Blessed Virgin Mary on the Mountain La Salette, on the 19th of September, 1846, The Pope in Red. Retrieved from http://www.thepopeinred.com/secret.htm, March 29, 2021.

& Associates, a Minnesota-based law firm that specializes in representing sex abuse survivors.[32]

Lawsuits by abuse victims have so far forced dioceses, parishes and religious orders in the United States to pay settlements totaling more than $3 billion. At least 19 have filed for bankruptcy protection. The diocesan at stake in the ongoing cases include cash, stocks, land and buildings, in addition to insurance payouts.[33]

What has been quite difficult to swallow and incredibly unbelievable or surprising, are these Marian visionaries talking about apocalyptic prophecies that contained messages of having apostasy inside the Catholic Church and the crown jewel of the seat of Rome threatened by Satan himself. I believe though that this is the very reason that Mary had appeared several times to reinforce her messages but since the message sounds quite revolting, throughout time, the message has been deemed impossible, implausible, ignored or acceptance refused. Still, somewhere in people's hearts, they know that full understanding of the messages from the Marian apparitions still has to be presented and perhaps, manifested. The La Salette was one of the firsts in a string of Mary's apparitions where apocalyptic prophecies were mentioned in relation to the Catholic Church.

Maximin and Melanie's Secrets

The children of La Salette obdurately refused to disclose the "secret" messages, until finally, in 1851, they were convinced to

---

[32] Lindsay Schnell. "Most priests accused of sexually abusing children were never sent to prison. Here's why." Retrieved from USA Today. https://www.usatoday.com/story/news/nation/2019/11/11/catholic-sex-abuse-why-dont-accused-priests-go-jail/3997022002/ March 29, 2021.

[33] "Report Reveals Widespread Sexual Abuse by Over 300 Priests in Pennsylvania" Retrieved from NPR. https://www.npr.org/2018/08/18/639698062/the-clergy-abuse-crisis-has-cost-the-catholic-church-3-billion, March 29, 2021.

write the secrets and send them to the Pope for his eyes only. Maximin wrote his secret in July, but several weeks later, at the behest of his friend M. Dausse, he wrote a prophetic fantasy which Dausse took to be authentic. Maximin later insisted that what he wrote was a fiction, given his inclination to react to those who would pester him with request for prophecies. This unfortunate practice of Maximin had damaged his credibility regarding authentic revelation. We should not discount however the consistent testimony of M. Dausse and all others who knew Maximin throughout his life and attested to his unassuming simplicity and guilelessness.

This youthful innocence exudes through the simple narrative of the authentic "secret" to Maximin, recovered from the Vatican archives in 1999.

Maximin wrote:

> *Here is what this Lady said to me:*

> *"If my people continue, what I will say to you will arrive earlier, if it changes a little, it will be a little later.*

> *Before all that arrives, great disorders will arrive, in the Church, and everywhere. Then, after (that), our Holy Father the Pope will be persecuted. His successor will be a pontiff that nobody expects.*

On a Wednesday, May 13, 1981, the attempted assassination of Pope John Paul II took place in St. Peter's Square in Vatican City. While entering the square, the Pope was shot and wounded by Mehmet Ali Agca who was apprehended immediately and later sentenced to life in prison by an Italian court. John Paul II later forgave Agca for the assassination attempt. At the pope's request, he was pardoned by Italian president Carlo Azeglio Ciampi and was deported to Turkey in June 2000.

John Paul II was followed directly by Cardinal Joseph Aloisius Ratzinger, who came to be known as Pope Benedict XVI. He served as head of the Church and sovereign of the Vatican City from 2005 until his resignation in 2013. He chose to be known by the title "pope emeritus" upon his resignation.

Since no one really expected Pope Benedict XVI to resign, the untimely calling for a papal enclave in 2013 came out with the pontiff that nobody expected. Born Jorge Mario Bergoglio, he chose to be named Pope Francis after St. Francis. Francis is the first pope to be a member of the Society of Jesus, the first from the Americas, the first from the Southern hemisphere and the first pope from outside Europe since Gregory III, a Syrian who reigned in the 8th century.

Melanie, the other La Salette visionary, who first talked about apocalyptic prophecies, naturally, would not have the proper reception from the Church authorities at her time. Finally, in 1879, she released a greatly augmented version of the secret, including new interpretations of the truest secret as well as completely new revelations unmentioned in the 1851 version. All these new embellishments were indiscriminately attributed to Our Lady of La Salette, resulting in an apocalyptic tract many times longer than the authentic secret submitted to the Pope in 1851. This tract contained prophecies that were in tension with the Catholic faith as it asserts that Rome would apostatize.

After years or moving from convent to convent and never progressing beyond the novitiate, Melanie stayed in Castellamare from 1867 onward. When new religious orders were formed at La Salette in 1878, Melanie claimed she was authorized to provide their rules and habits. This request was denied by the bishop and later by the Pope himself in an interview with Melanie. In reaction to this thorough rejection by the Church hierarchy, Melanie wrote a new tract, full of bitter invective against a supposedly faithless clergy. Not contrary to faith and morals in the narrow sense, it received an imprimatur. In 1880 however, the Holy Office forbade her to write further tracts. A few copies of 1879 tract was circulated, and it was published again more widely in 1904. A third printing in 1922, with a new imprimatur, finally resulted in Rome's inclusion of the tract on the Index of Prohibited Books in 1923. Note however that the condemned 1922 version is nothing more than a simple reprinting of Melanie's original text of 1879, so Melanie's original text is what is being condemned, that Rome would apostatize. This judgment naturally supersedes the imprimatur of any local bishop, and as Cardinal Ratzinger has stated, the Index retains its moral force for Catholics, notwithstanding the fact that the list is no longer updated.

To this day, the condemned tract is widely reprinted. Relying on the authority of the imprimatur and on the status of La Salette as an approved apparition, many well-meaning Catholics have come to believe that this anticlerical diatribe is actually endorsed by the Church. Leaning towards schism, traditionalists find in it vindication of their belief that Rome had in fact lost the faith, as have most of the world's bishops. On the other hand, some sober-minded people may recoil from the booklet's wild claims and may come to disbelieve in La Salette and in Marian apparitions more generally.

The definition of apostasy is the abandonment or renunciation of a religious or political belief. Maximin's prophecy of "a pope not expected" and Melanie's "the church will apostatize" may have found its combination in Pope Francis' writing of the Amoris Laetitia.

Not to be confusing but let me add quickly a verse from my blog article reflecting the Fatima prophecy:

> *"Next year, 2017, will be the centennial. I have also come to know to confirm my suspicions that, St. Lucia herself who kept the third secret has said*

*one of the signs of the final battle between Mary,
God's mother and Satan will be about marriage
and family, which is quite a very sensitive topic
these days.*

*The other thing that was a give-away for me was I
believe it was prophesied that the third secret will
be revealed during a Year of Redemption. I am
looking for the actual texts but I could not find it.
Well, 2016 had been designated by Pope Francis as
the Jubilee Year of Mercy so that would be a Year
of Redemption."*

That would be like four for four. Four checks for four prophecies.

Dated March 19, 2016, Amoris Laetitia (The Joy of Love) is a post-synodal apostolic exhortation by Pope Francis addressing the pastoral care of families, actually released on April 8 2016, following the Synods on the Family held in 2014 and 2015.

The exhortation covers a broad range of topics related to marriage and family life as well as the contemporary challenges faced by families throughout the world. Amoris Laetitia encourages both pastors and members of the laity to accompany and care for families and others in situations of particular need. It also includes an extended reflection on the meaning of love in the day-to-day reality of family life.

Controversy arose following the publication of Amoris Laetitia regarding whether Chapter 8 of the exhortation had changed the Catholic Church's sacramental discipline concerning access to the sacraments of Reconciliation and Eucharist for divorced couples who have civilly remarried.

On 29 June 2016, forty-five Catholics presented a letter to the Dean of the College of Cardinals, Cardinal Angelo Sodano. The letter expressed claim to find 12 heretical propositions and 8 propositions falling under lesser theological censures.

On September 2016, four cardinals (Raymond Burke, Carlo Caffara, Walter Brandmuller and Joachim Meisner), in a private letter, asked Pope Francis to clarify regarding Chapter 8 of Amoris Laetitia. The letter contained five questions (dubia) and requested a yes or no answer. After not receiving a response from Pope Francis, the cardinals then publicized this letter on November 2016. Their questions are based on "whether there are now circumstances under which divorced and remarried persons can receive communion, whether there are still absolute moral norms that prohibit Catholics from taking certain acts and how the pope understands Catholic teaching on the role of conscience in making moral decisions."[34]

German philosopher Robert Spaemann and British academic Joseph Shaw have expressed support for the initiative of the cardinals. Cardinal George Pell, Prefect of the Vatican Secretariat for the Economy asked: "How can you disagree with a question?" In December 2016, the head of the Congregation for the Doctrine of the Faith Cardinal Gerard Muller, stated that he does not believe that the doctrine on communion can change while declaring that it was not the role of the Congregation to engage in the controversy.

Oxford philosopher John Finnis and theologian Germain Grisez also expressed their concern in a detailed letter, requesting the pope to condemn eight positions against the Catholic faith "that are being supported, or likely will be, by the misuse" of *Amoris Laetitia*.

However, according to Antonio Spadaro, a Jesuit priest who is also a close adviser to Pope Francis, the controversial questions on communion were already answered. Archbishop of Brisbane Mark Coleridge said that prelates supporting the *dubia* are not addressing reality. They are pursuing a "false clarity that comes because you don't address reality". In line with this point, it has been suggested that Pope Francis declined to answer the *dubia*

---

[34] Ibid.

because he wants to emphasize a more humane, pastoral approach and de-emphasize the demand for legal clarity.

Cardinal Caffarra reiterated that after *Amoris Laetitia* "only a blind man could deny there's great confusion, uncertainty and insecurity in the Church." [35]

In January 2017, three Kazakhstan bishops issued a joint statement advocating prayer that Pope Francis will "confirm the unchanging praxis of the Church with regard to the truth of the indissolubility of marriage."[36] They strongly held that some of the recent "pastoral guidelines contradict the universal tradition of the Catholic Church."[37]

In February 2017, several confraternities of priests, in the United States, the United Kingdom, Ireland and Australia, asked to formally clarify Chapter 8 of *Amoris Laetitia*.

On February 14, 2017, the head of the Pontifical Council for Legislative Texts, Cardinal Francesco Coccopalmerio, authored a 50-page booklet stating that Chapter 8 of *Amoris Laetitia* allows access to the sacraments for the divorced and civilly remarried only if they recognize that their situation is sinful and desire to change it. He wrote that this intention to change, even if the couple cannot do so immediately, "is exactly the theological element that allows absolution and access to the Eucharist as long as – I repeat – there is the impossibility of immediately changing the situation of sin."[38] The Pontifical Council for Legislative Texts interprets Church law.

On May 6, 2017, Carlo Caffara, on behalf of the four cardinals sought a papal audience with Pope Francis. He stated his intent on a private hand-delivered letter. Caffarra disclosed that "interpretations of some objectively ambiguous passages" of *Amoris Laetitia* are not merely divergent from, but contrary to,

---

[35] Ibid.
[36] Ibid.
[37] Ibid.
[38] Ibid.

the permanent Magisterium of the Church. In June, again, having not yet received a response from Pope Francis, the cardinals publicized the letter.

Cardinal Meisner died on July 5, 2017, and Cardinal Caffarra followed on September 6, 2017.

In July 2017, a group of 40 (now over 260) Catholic clergy, lay scholars, and theologians signed and presented to Pope Francis a 25-page document entitled "Correctio filialis de haeresibus propagatis" (A Filial Correction Concerning the Propagation of Heresies). The document states that certain passages from *Amoris Laetitia* and other "words, deeds, and omissions" of Pope Francis "are serving to propagate heresies". The document had 62 signatories when it was made public in September after the group received no reply.[39]

In September 2017, Pope Francis told a gathering of Jesuits in Colombia that Amoris Laetitia need to be read from beginning to end. He also stressed that the morality of Amoris Laetitia is a Thomist.

A year after the publication of the dubia, Cardinal Burke made a "final plea" to Pope Francis, mentioning the "continually worsening" gravity of the situation in the Church in the wake of the exhortation.[40]

On 31 December 2017, three bishops of Kazakhstan, including Bishop Athanasius Schneider, presented a "Profession of Immutable Truths about Sacramental Marriage". The Profession indicated that some pastoral guidelines issued by bishops that allow the divorced and civilly remarried to receive the sacraments of Penance and Holy Communion have caused confusion among the Catholic faithful and clergy. The Profession states: "An approval or legitimation of the violation of the sacredness of

---

[39] "Amoris Letitia." Wikipedia. Retrieved from https://en.wikipedia.org/wiki/Amoris_laetitia. March 30, 2021.
[40] Ibid.

the marriage bond, even indirectly through the mentioned new sacramental discipline, seriously contradicts God's express will and His commandment".[41] Later, one month after its release, seven other bishops, including Cardinal Janis Pujats and Archbishops Carlo Maria Viganò and Luigi Negri, had added their names to the Profession.

Early in 2018, Father Kevin J. Flannery, professor at Pontifical Gregorian University, and Father V. Thomas Berg, professor at Saint Joseph's Seminary, published an article in Nova et Vetera challenging *Amoris Laetitia's* reliance on the writings of Thomas Aquinas.

In January 2018, Cardinal Pietro Parolin, Vatican Secretary of State, stated that *Amoris Laetitia* "resulted from a new paradigm which Pope Francis is carrying forward with wisdom, prudence, and patience," and that difficulties surrounding the document "besides some aspects of content, are due to this change of attitude the Pope is asking of us. Cardinal Blase Cupich of Chicago, on the other hand, stated on February 2018, that *Amoris Laetitia* "represents a major shift in our ministerial approach that is nothing short of revolutionary." Referring to critics of *Amoris Laetitia*, Cupich said, "instead of actually attending to the present reality of people's lives today in all its complexity, they limit their scope to an idealistic understanding of marriage and family."[42]

In February 2018 Cardinal Müller replied that, when understood in the sense of a "fundamental change in theoretical forms of thought and social behavior," there can be no paradigm shifts in the Catholic faith. Müller wrote that "a paradigm shift, by which the Church takes on the criteria of modern society to be assimilated by it, constitutes not a development, but a corruption."[43]

---

[41] Ibid.

[42] Ibid.

[43] Ibid.

In August 2018, Pope Francis wrote to English author Stephen Walford, giving the following explanation for *Amoris Laetitia*:

"The Exhortation *Amoris Laetitia* is a unified whole which means that, in order to understand its message, it must be read in its entirety and from the beginning. This is because there is a development both of theological reflection and of the way in which problems are approached. It cannot be considered a *vademecum* on different issues. If the Exhortation is not read in its entirety and in the order it is written, it will either not be understood or it will be distorted. Over the course of the Exhortation, current and concrete problems are dealt with: the family in today's world, the education of children, marriage preparation, families in difficulty, and so on; these are treated with a hermeneutic that comes from the whole document which is the magisterial hermeneutic of the Church, always in continuity (without ruptures), yet always maturing. With respect to the problems that involve ethical situations, the Exhortation follows the classical doctrine of St. Thomas Aquinas."[44]

In the same month, Cardinal Scola, an Italian theologian and philosopher, publicly expressed for the first time his opposition to the communion of the divorced and civilly remarried unless they live in complete continence. According to Scola, the removal of this prohibition would be a break with the doctrine, because it is "not a punishment that can be taken away or reduced, but is inherent in the very character of Christian marriage."

A year before all that, I remember standing frozen like Lot's wife in front of the television in our office. The Supreme Court just announced that it was striking down all state bans on same-sex marriage and was legalizing it in all fifty states. The Supreme Court required states to honor out-of-state same sex marriage licenses in the case Obergefell v. Hodges. There was a huge celebration on television because now, gays, lesbians, bisexuals

---

[44] Ibid.

and transgenders can now apply for a marriage license and get married.

It did not however come without a fight and without cutting some corners somewhere.

In 2000, the State of California adopted Proposition 22, which forbade recognition or licensing of same-sex marriages in the state, as an ordinary statute. In March 2004, San Francisco Mayor Gavin Newsom directed the licensing of same-sex marriages based on the state's equal protection clause, prompted also by recent events which included George W. Bush's proposed constitutional ban, a possible legal case by Campaign for California Families (CCF) and a Supreme Court of Massachusetts ruling deeming same-sex marriage bans unconstitutional and permitting them from May, 2004. While only lasting a month before being overruled, this was supported by other cities such as San Jose, gained global attention and led to the case In *re Marriage Cases*, in which Proposition 22 was found (San Francisco County Superior Court, March 14, 2005) and confirmed upon appeal (California Supreme Court, May 15, 2008) to be unconstitutional.[45]

Proposition 8 was created then by opponents of same-sex marriage prior to the final ruling on *In re Marriage Cases* as a voter ballot initiative, to be voted on at the time of the November 2008 elections. The wordings of Proposition 8 were precisely the same as Proposition 22, except that it was repositioned as a State constitutional amendment rather than a legislative statute. It was then able to bypass the ruling from *In re Marriage Cases*. It did not influence domestic partnerships in California, nor (following subsequent legal rulings) did it reverse same-sex marriages that had been performed during the interim period of May to November 2008. (after In re Marriage cases but before Proposition 8)

---

[45] "Same-sex Marriage" Wikipedia. Retrieved from https://en.wikipedia.org/wiki/Same-sex_marriage. April 5, 2021.

Proposition 8 took effect immediately on November 5, 2008, the day after the elections. Demonstrations and protests occurred across the state and nation. Same-sex couples and government entities, including couples who had married before then, filed numerous lawsuits with the California Supreme Court challenging the proposition's validity and effect on previously administered same-sex marriages. In Strauss v. Horton, the California Supreme Court upheld Proposition 8. It, however, allowed the existing same-sex marriages to stand (under the grandfather clause principle). Justice Carlos Moreno dissented that exceptions to the equal protection clause could not be made by any majority since its whole purpose was to protect minorities against the will of majority.)

Although upheld in State court, Proposition 8 was ruled unconstitutional by the federal courts. In Perry v. Schwarzenegger, US District Court Judge Vaughn Walker overturned Proposition 8 on August 4, 2010. He ruled that it violated both the Due Process and Equal Protection clauses of the US Constitution. Walker issued a stay (an injunction) against enforcing Proposition 8 and a stay to determine suspension of his ruling pending appeal. Although it had agreed to anyway, the State of California did not appeal the ruling leaving the initiative proponents and one county to seek an appeal. There were two issues here: one, Judge Vaughn Walker NEVER CONFIRMED PUBLICLY that he is gay. He only did so after leaving the bench. It was a year later, in an interview 2011, that Judge Walker admitted that he's gay, that he has been in a relationship with a male doctor for 10 years.[46] He should have had the ethicality to recuse himself from the case. It's like being a native American and the case is about native Americans. How can one rule ethically if the issue affects the persona of the judge?

---

[46] "Vaughn Walker." Wikipedia. Retrieved from https://en.wikipedia.org/wiki/Vaughn_Walker. April 5, 2021.

Secondly, the Attorney General then, now Vice-President Kamala Harris refused to defend the State Law, even though it went to the nation's highest court. Harris, a San Francisco Democrat, had already decided that Proposition 8 violated the Constitution, and the U.S. Supreme Court had described marriage as a fundamental right 14 times since 1888.[47] She justified her action by saying "it's well within the authority vested in me as the elected attorney general to use the discretion of my office to make decisions about how we will use our resources and what issue we will weigh in or not," she said leaving it up to the traditional marriage supporters to defend Prop 8 all the way up to the Supreme Court. They argued that the initiative process is well within states' rights.

On appeal, a Ninth Circuit Court of Appeals panel ruled the county had no right of appeal and asked the California Supreme Court to rule whether the proponents of Prop 8 had the right to appeal (known as "standing") if the State did not do so. The California Supreme Court ruled they did. The Ninth Circuit affirmed the federal district court's decision on February 7, 2012 but the injunction remained in place as appeals continued to the U.S. Supreme Court which heard oral arguments in the appeal Hollingsworth v Perry on March 26, 2013. On June 26, 2013, the Supreme Court dismissed the appeal and ruled that the Ninth Circuit had erred in allowing previous appeal, since in line with Article III of the Constitution and in many prior cases unanimous on the point, being an initiative proponent is not enough by itself to have federal court standing appeal or appeal a ruling in federal court. This left the original federal district court ruling against Proposition 8 as the final outcome and same sex marriages resumed almost immediately afterwards.

---

[47] "Attorney General Kamala Harris turns down Prop 8 defense before Supreme Court" ABC7.com. Retrieved from https://abc7.com/archive/9042429/. April 6, 2021.

The Roman Catholic Church, as well as a Roman Catholic lay organization, the Knights of Columbus, firmly supported the measure. The bishops of the California Catholic Conference released a statement supporting the proposition. Some archbishops raised funds and spoke for Proposition 8. Knights of Columbus donated more than $1.4 million to Proposition 8.[48] The Order was the largest financial supporter of the successful effort to maintain a legal definition of marriage as the union of one man and one woman.

Between January 2012 and February 2014, plaintiffs in Michigan, Ohio, Kentucky and Tennessee filed federal district court case that culminated in Obergefell v Hodges. After all district courts ruled for the plaintiffs, the rulings were appealed to the Sixth Circuit. In November 2014, following a series of appeals court ruling that year from the Fourth, Seventh, Ninth and Tenth Circuits that state-level bans on same-marriage were unconstitutional, the Sixth Circuit ruled that it was bound by Baker v Nelson and found such bans to be constitutional. This created a split between circuits and led to a Supreme Court review.

On June 26, 2015, the landmark civil rights case, Obergefell overturned Baker. In Obergefell v Hodges, the Supreme Court of the United States ruled that the fundamental right to marry is guaranteed to same-sex couples by both the Due Process Clause and the Equal Protection Clause of the Fourteenth Amendment to the United States Constitution.[49]

On April 4, 2021, Los Angeles, which belonged to the Ninth Circuit registered on top of the coronavirus cases nationally at 1,220,893 only to be followed by Maricopa County at 525,002.[50]

[48] "Same-sex Marriage" Wikipedia. Retrieved from https://en.wikipedia.org/wiki/Same-sex_marriage. April 5, 2021.
[49] "Obergefell v Hodges" Wikipedia. Retrieved from https://en.wikipedia.org/wiki/Obergefell_v._Hodges. April 5, 2021.
[50] "Covid-19 US Cases by County" Johns Hopkins University. Retrieved from https://coronavirus.jhu.edu/us-map. April 4, 2021.

The deaths in Los Angeles were recorded at 23,236. Followed by Kings County with 9,709. The whole of California recorded cases of 3,675,191 while the deaths rattled at 59,614.[51]

It may all seem coincidental or perhaps not.

The La Salette Popes

There were four popes during the time of the La Salette visionaries. At the time of the La Salette apparition in 1846, there was just a new pope, Pope Pius IX, born Giovanni Maria Mastai Ferretti. He was born on May 13, 1792 and died February 7, 1878. He was the head of the Catholic Church from 1846 to 1878, the longest papal reign. He was notable for convening the First Vatican Council in 1868. He was also noted for permanently losing control of the Papal States in 1870 to the Kingdom of Italy. He refused to leave the Vatican City, proclaiming himself a "prisoner of the Vatican."

In his encyclical, *Ubi primum*, Pius IX emphasized Mary's role in salvation. In 1854, he propagated the dogma of the Immaculate Conception, articulating a long-held Catholic belief that Mary, the Mother of God, was conceived without original sin. His 1864 Syllabus of Errors was a strong condemnation against liberalism, modernism, moral relativism, secularization and separation of church and state. Pius IX definitely reasserted Catholic teaching in favor of the establishment of the Catholic faith as the state religion wherever viable. His appeal for financial support resulted in the successful revival of donations known as Peter's Pence. He consolidated power in the church in the Holy See and the Roman Curia, while also clearly defining the Pope's doctrinal authority. His chief legacy is the dogma of papal infallibility, that by virtue of the promise of Jesus to Peter, the pope, acting as supreme teacher and under certain conditions, cannot err when he teaches in matters of faith and morals.

---

[51] Ibid.

John Paul II declared Pius IX Venerable on 6 July 1985 and beatified him on 3 September 2000. Pius IX was assigned the liturgical feast day of February 7. It was the date of his death.

At that time, Melanie wrote her 1879 tract that "Rome would apostatize." When she was forbidden to write anymore tracts in 1880, it was already Pope Leo XIII who was Pope.

Pope Leo XIII, born Vincenzo Gioacchino Raffaele Luigi Pecci on March 2, 1810 and died on July 20, 1903. Pope Leo XIII was the oldest pope (reigning until the age of 93), with the exception of Pope Benedict XVI as emeritus pope. He also had the third longest confirmed pontificate, behind those of Pius IX, his immediate predecessor and John Paul II.

Pope Leo's influence on the Mariology of the Catholic Church was that he promoted both rosary and scapular. He issued a record of eleven papal encyclicals on the rosary, earning him the title as the "Rosary Pope." In addition, he approved two new Marian scapulars and was the first pope to fully embrace the concept of Mary as Mediatrix. In Catholic Mariology, the title Mediatrix refers to the intercessory role of the Blessed Virgin Mary as a mediator in the salvific redemption by her son Jesus Christ and the belief that He bestows graces through her. Mediatrix is an ancient title that has been used by many saints since at least the 5th century.

Pope Leo XIII was also famous for his vision of seeing a conversation between God and Satan, whereby Satan asked for 100 years to destroy the Catholic Church.

By the time, Melanie's tracts of prophecies had a third printing in 1922 and were included in the condemned books in 1923, the Pope at that time was Pope Benedict XV. Pope Benedict XV's legacy was his attempts to build peace among countries during the time of World War I.

CHAPTER 15

Pope Leo XIII Prophetic Vision

"On 13 October, 1884 Pope Leo XIII, just after celebrating Mass, turned pale and collapsed as though dead. Those standing nearby rushed to his side. They found him alive but the pontiff looked frightened. He then recounted having a vision of Satan approaching the throne of God, boasting that he could destroy the Church.

According to Pope Leo XIII the Lord reminded him that his Church was imperishable. Satan then replied, *"Grant me one century and more power of those who will serve me, and I will destroy it."*[52] Our Lord granted him 100 years.

The Lord then revealed the events of the 20th century to Leo XIII. He saw wars, immorality, genocide and apostasy on a large scale. Immediately following this disturbing vision, he sat down and wrote the prayer to St. Michael. For decades it was prayed at Mass until the 1960's. Like many of the Church's spiritual defenses, it was discontinued in the second half of the 20th century.

A number of versions about the vision have appeared over the years. Pope Leo himself never spoke in public or in writing about the incident. Joe Tremblay, in his 2013 article the *100 Years*

---

[52] "God's Chat with the Devil" Catholic Stand, May 18, 2018 issue, Retrieved from https://catholicstand.com/gods-chat-devil-popeleo/, March 31, 2021.

Test, writes *"the pope turned pale and collapsed as though dead.*[53]*" Tradition in Action* offers another version claiming that Leo added "in the midst of the horror (of the vision) the Archangel St. Michael appeared and cast Satan and his legions into the abyss of hell. Father William Saunders, in his 2003 article, *"The Prayer to St. Michael,"* stated that there were several attending Cardinals who found *"the pope with no pulse....and the Holy Father was feared dead (and then) suddenly, Pope Leo awoke and said, 'What a horrible picture I was permitted to see!"*[54] Fr Saunders expressed that God gave Satan the choice of one century in which to do his worst work against the Church...the devil chose the twentieth century. *"So troubling was the vision, that the Pope composed the Prayer to St. Michael in which he pleaded "defend us in battle!" and to "be our protection against the wickedness and snares of the devil."*[55] The pope instructed that the prayer be recited at the end of each Lower Mass. Pope Paul VI ended the mandatory prayer in 1964.

Historical investigations gave the first public story in a 1933 German newspaper about the prayer to the Archangel St. Michael. One year later, Fr. Bers, a German writer, claimed that after an extensive search he could find no mention of the vision. A 1955 edition of the Roman journal *Ephemerides Liturgicae,* cited Father Domenic Pechenino, who worked at the Vatican during Leo XIII's papacy and who claimed in 1947 that he witnessed the event. The same article quotes Cardinal Nasalli Rocca di Corneliamo (1872-1952) relating that Leo's private secretary, "Monsignor Rinaldo Angeli ...(claimed) Leo had seen a vision of demonic spirits who were congregating on the Eternal City (Rome) which inspired him to write the Saint Michael prayer."[56]

---

[53] "God's Chat with the Devil" Catholic Stand, May 18, 2018 issue, Retrieved from https://catholicstand.com/gods-chat-devil-popeleo/, March 31, 2021.

[54] Ibid.

[55] Ibid.

[56] Ibid.

Emmett O' Regan in his blog *Prophecy of Pope Leo XIII* suggested that before 1933, the story must have "originally circulated orally among the Vatican staff and employees." Neither Father Pechenino nor Monsignor Angeli cited the fainting and deathlike trance of the Pope. O' Regan writes that Pechenino stated, "*we saw him raise his head and stare at something above the (Mass) Celebrant's head. He was staring noiselessly, without batting an eye. His expression was one of horror and awe; the color and look of his face changing rapidly. Something unusual and grave was happening to him... (and then) coming to his senses...he headed for private office. An hour later, he handed the Secretary of the Congregation of Rights the Prayer to St. Michael and told him to send it out to all the ordinaries of the world.*"[57] Pechenino also did not recall what year the incident occurred.

---

[57] "God's Chat with the Devil" Catholic Stand, May 18, 2018 issue, Retrieved from https://catholicstand.com/gods-chat-devil-popeleo/, March 31, 2021.

CHAPTER 16

Our Lady of Fatima

From the blog Mary Z Rewriting the Faith. Writing # 1

Godlessness Angers God

The Story of Fatima and Isaiah's Apocalyptic Visions

Isaiah 29:16 *"They turn everything upside down. Which is more important, the potter or the clay? Can something a man has made tell him, "You didn't make me"? Or can it say to him, "You don't know what you're doing?"*[58]

Isaiah 26:9-10. *"At night, I long for you with my heart; When you judge the earth and its people, they will all learn what justice is. Even though, you are kind to wicked men, they never learn to do what is right. Even here in a land of righteous people they still do wrong; they refuse to recognize your greatness.*[59]

---

[58] "The Good News Bible. American Bible Society. New York. p. 766
[59] Ibid., p. 766

For some reason last week, I felt inclined to spend a holy hour at the Adoration Chapel in our church. I am still growing in the spiritual sense so that was kind of an unusual draw since at the most, I get to spend about 20 minutes praying and then I get restless and finish my prayers.

At the entrance of the small adoration chapel, there is a counter and some pigeonhole boxes where prayer cards, pamphlets and booklets are often placed for people to take and use. Somebody had left a magazine about the apparitions of Our Lady of Fatima. I took interest in the magazine. Since I am already quite familiar with the story of Fatima, I focused on reading a very latter chapter about "Lucia's mission." It talked about how in the beginning, the newly assigned Bishop in the revived diocese that covered Fatima, made sure of the sincerity of the message of Our Lady's apparition. The bishop then sent Lucia to a convent and hid her under an assumed name. The bishop's rationale was that if the messages about the Lady was true, the miracles and cures that had already taken place would continue, if not, the false devotion would just extinguish its fire naturally. The bishop's actions hardly deterred the Lady from talking to Lucia about her messages and her promises. Lucia was shown the vision of the Blessed Mother's bleeding heart covered with thorns. Our Lady and the Child Jesus who both appeared to Lucia, asked for the reparation and consolation from people's offenses by their sins. Actually, Lucia being in the convent, just made her more accessible to the religious hierarchy and guidance through her institution. The most significant point of the chapter was that as Lucia had relayed the message that Our Lady of Fatima is asking for the consecration of Russia, where godlessness was spilling off the brim, the church leaders at that time kept misunderstanding that it was meant as consecration of the whole world.

ANGELITA FELIXBERTO

From the blog Mary Z Rewriting the Faith. Writing # 2

The Last Secret of Fatima, Visions of Mary and the Revelation

In Genesis 3: we find the fall of Adam and Eve from grace and the beginning of the enmity between the serpent and the woman.

"The Lord God asked the woman, "Why did you do this?" She replied, "The snake tricked me into eating it." Then the Lord God said to the snake, "You will be punished for this: you alone of all the animals must bear this curse: From now on you will crawl on your belly, and you will have to eat dust as long as you live. I will make you and the woman hate each other; her offspring and yours will always be enemies. Her offspring will crush your head, and you will bite their heel." Genesis 3:13-15.

In Matthew 16:18, Jesus appointed Simon Peter as the foundation of His church. "And I tell you, you are Peter, and on this rock, I will build my church, and the gates of hell shall not prevail against it."[60]

That statement of Jesus Christ, that the gates of hell shall not prevail against it was challenged by Satan to be put to the test for a period of a century.

On October 13, 1884, Pope Leo XIII, just after celebrating Mass, turned pale and collapsed as though dead. The people standing by rushed to his side, found him alive but looked frightened. He then recounted a vision of Satan approaching the throne of God taunting that he could destroy the Church.

According to Pope Leo XIII, the Lord reminded Satan that His Church cannot be prevailed against. Satan boasted, "Grant me one century and more power of those who will serve me and I

---

[60] The Good News Bible. American Bible Society. New York. p.4.

92

will destroy it."[61] Our Lord agreed to give him the requested time. The Lord then revealed the horrible events to come within the 20th century to Pope Leo XIII. Wars, immorality, genocide and apostasy on a large scale was envisioned by the pontiff. After the revelation, he sat down and wrote the prayer to St. Michael. The prayer for St. Michael's protection was prayed at Mass until the 1960's. It was discontinued in the latter part of the 20th century.

From my readings and research, no one can really pinpoint when will that 100 years of Satan's time frame of challenge destroying God's Church begins or ends. For most people, it was a shot in the dark or a moving target. From my curious readings about the promise of Our Lady of Fatima, it said that the Church will not easily reveal the "Third Secret" of the Fatima because it would be quite too hot to handle at any one point in the church history. There were so many approximations and there were so many learned writings trying to interpret the history, the context, the meaning and everything else in between all the events and circumstances to unravel the meaning of the Our Lady of Fatima's secret. You can and you will be able to read, as I have just read, the significance of the secret of Fatima and how it may have related to Pope Leo XIII's message way back when, but maybe none would sound as silly as an intuitive mystic inspiration. And I assure you, many will try to benefit commercially from this knowledge, as false prophets and entrepreneurs always fill in the landscape of politics, religion, materialism. For some unscrupulous people, God is like a movie star who is subject to the economy of the media.

The one statement that guided me about the Third Secret of Fatima is this: "evil will be within or inside the Church." Most people would think it would be a particular person, individual or

---

[61] "Has Pope Leo XIII's 100-Year Vision Reached its Terminus?" The Five Beasts. "The Message of Fatima" Congregation for the Doctrine of the Faith. Retrieved from https://www.vatican.va/roman_curia/congregations/cfaith/documents/rc_con_cfaith_doc_20000626_message-fatima_en.html. April 6, 2021.

*character who is supernaturally endowed with evil powers or in disguise. **Next year, 2017, will be the centennial. I have also come to know to confirm my suspicions that, St. Lucia herself who kept the third secret has said one of the signs of the final battle between Mary, God's mother and Satan will be about marriage and family, which is quite a very sensitive topic these days.***

The other thing that was a give-away for me was I believe it was prophesied that the third secret will be revealed during a Year of Redemption. I am looking for the actual texts but I could not find it. Well, 2016 had been designated by Pope Francis as the Jubilee Year of Mercy so that would be a Year of Redemption.

"The third part of the secret refers to Our Lady's words: 'If not [Russia] will spread her errors throughout the world, causing wars and persecutions of the Church. The good will be martyred; the Holy Father will have much to suffer; various nations will be annihilated' (13-VII-1917). [62]

The third part of the secret is a symbolic revelation, referring to this part of the Message, conditioned by whether we accept or not what the Message itself asks of us: "If my requests are heeded, Russia will be converted, and there will be peace; if not, she will spread her errors throughout the world, etc." [63]

The symbolism of Russia is the Godlessness of the many inhabitants of the earth. Throughout my lifetime, Russia has symbolized anything that goes against the grains of being a society that respects God. In Revelations. In Revelations 12:9 evil was noted with the Devil as the dragon and the ancient serpent as Satan. Revelations 13:4, "Everyone worshiped the dragon because he had given his authority to the beast. They worshiped the beast also,

---

[62] "The Message of Fatima" Congregation for the Doctrine of the Faith. Retrieved from https://www.vatican.va/roman_curia/congregations/cfaith/documents/rc_con_cfaith_doc_20000626_message-fatima_en.html. April 6, 2021.

[63] Ibid.

saying "Who is like the beast? Who can fight against it?"[64] The beast, from my divinely inspired interpretation is not a physical but a symbolic beast of anything that goes against God, like right now. This includes atheism, secularism, homosexuality, perversion of sexuality, violations against human life, trampling of religious freedom, extremist Islam, etc." To me that is the beast, which seems unconquerable.

In the third message of Fatima, there is a mention of those "entrusted."

*"Mother of all individuals and peoples, you know all their sufferings and hopes. In your motherly heart you feel all the struggles between good and evil, between light and darkness, that convulse the world: accept the plea which we make in the Holy Spirit directly to your heart, and embrace with the love of the Mother and Handmaid of the Lord those who most await this embrace, and **also those whose act of entrustment you too await in a particular way.** Take under your motherly protection the whole human family, which with affectionate love we entrust to you, O Mother. May the time of peace and freedom, the time of truth, of justice and of hope dawn on everyone."[65]*

I have a relationship which is kind of a symbolic of that "entrustment." My colleagues in my religious organization have nicknamed me, "Mary" and my significant other as, "John." Since we are both religious, they have associated our meeting with the disciple John and Mary his mother at the foot of the cross. Mary was actually "entrusted" to the disciple John by Jesus, presuming that her spouse Joseph had already passed away at that time, since there were no longer mention of him in the Bible.

Also, from my readings about Fatima, I read about this miraculous 54-day Rosary novena which I have suggested. I had that thought that I should join the rosary simultaneous with

---

[64] The Good News Bible. American Bible Society. New York. p.344-345.
[65] Ibid.

my prayers. On the first night of the rosary, I believe I saw a vision of Mary, telling me that I should also pray simultaneously during these 54 days of the Rosary, and that will be my personal sacrifice to be offered together with the novena to make it more efficacious. Every night, I listen to the Gregorian chant of the complete Holy Rosary, and as I progressed, I have started to have visions and immediate thoughts of reply that the Blessed Mother and I are pretty much conversing. The uncanny or unbelievable part of it is that, what we normally talked about, would be in timing with what something for discussion during the course of the next day.

The Blessed Mother had asked me to have more people offer their rosary prayers so that she can bring these prayers to the Heavenly Father and intercede for us. My sacrifice would be to feel the heavy load of the Blessed Mother's heart and she said that that will be our bond. She told me she will teach how to be more patient with anything offensive to me and to pray for the salvation of those who offend me. Every night, I see a vision of almost every conceivable evil that humans can act upon, e.g., people being rounded up for torture, seeing men stabbing other, people being beheaded, women being raped, babies, dead or alive, being taken from the woman who has just given birth to the baby, soldiers dying or dead on the trenches, children, women and men dying from hunger and poverty, women running in the middle of the night to elude captors, women slaves being chained and so on and so forth. Speaking with the Blessed Mother in my vision would bring me to an ecstatic state, where I rock myself back and forth because the good feeling is such prolonged overwhelming, but the other side of the coin is the painful sights and feelings of being right there during the scene where evil was committed, except people cannot see me. I would feel like really drained after the visions. The Blessed Mother had actually asked me to write down my visions. As time went on, I had asked the Blessed Mother, just via thoughts, if I should really see all these things, but then she told me,

"Just keep looking." At this time, we have already developed quite a comfortable relationship with each other from our conversations during my visions. At the time, the recent Italian earthquake was shortly about to occur, through my thoughts she had asked me to post the pictures of Our Lady of La Salette crying. Since I was too tired, I also posted a couple of pictures of animals yawning heading to sleep. I did not realize until the morning after that there was this terrible earthquake in Italy where almost the whole town had disappeared. I was engrossed in reading about the prophecies of Our Lady of La Salette which I am not sure if everything had been fulfilled since this was in the late 1800's.

I have an inspired interpretation of particular segments of the Revelation. From what the Lady had told me, the time of reaping and judgment had already started. There were particular numbers on the text of Revelation that seemed highlighted to me, which was a crucial 42 months from when this "perfect storm" battle between Our Lady and Satan will occur, as prophesied in Genesis and Revelations. I do know from my vision that heaven and earth will still exist but the transition between the old and the new world will be very chaotic both with man-made and natural disasters. I saw in my vision like a multitude of angels, like an army size, descending from heaven and helping out living people. I saw on separate events, an elderly man, being assisted by an angel, the help of which was oblivious and the angel invisible to the men.

I have asked the Blessed Mother what we can do and if she can give me more information. She said, "Pray. Pray. Pray" because this battle is really between her and Satan but she needs prayers because the Trinity and her wants to save more souls. She also said that not everything will be revealed all at once.

Figuring out the numbers mentioned in the Bible, it looked like one day for God is one year for people. This great "day" of battle between Mary and the serpent, would probably start the year of 2017, where the first apparition of Our Lady of Fatima will have its centennial, and the 100 years given to Satan should end. The year 2017 was marked with a full solar eclipse. 1917 was marked with a miracle of the Sun, while a hundred years later came the full solar eclipse where the Sun's corona was visible and everything stood still as people watched the solar eclipse pass by. From Revelations, the new heaven and earth will have peace for 1000 years. I interpreted this new heaven and earth as a renewed nature of the world where God's will, peace, love and joy reign. After that 1000 years, the Devil will be let out for some time again.

Previously, I have made personal notes of my inspired interpretation of the Book of Revelation, which I will share later. I have honestly not figured out when will that 42 months of turmoil and chaos and darkness will start. I do know there is a full eclipse scheduled next year, and as what the Muslims had been waiting for that also came to me from a vision, a lunar and a solar eclipse, supposed to be during the time of Ramadan. The dates of Ramadan are not exactly fixed but it is close to the months of May and June I believe. However, there are two months next year which will have both lunar and solar eclipse at the same time. Also, the coming solar eclipse in August next year will be totally full.

I also have not received revelations yet about the seven plagues that will come about. What I do know is that the reaping for judgment had already begun. Some of the information were given to me, or I have to request for it. Sometimes, even if I ask for it, Mary would tell me that things will be revealed to me in due time.

I just want to say, no one has to believe me for these visions. This intimate very maternal but also friendly relationship with Mary includes like being a mutual confidant to each other. I even tell her when I lose to my fiery temper and she would tell me to let the anger subside and she will help me become more patient because I will share the burdens in her heart as my personal sacrifice.

The other thing I know too is that one of the amazing experiences is that whatever Mary and I were discussing tend to *be one of the readings or homilies the next day. It was so intriguing and just to see the face of Mary in my mental eye brings me to ecstasy with her incomparable radiant beauty, and her graceful composure, humility, meekness, calmness and peacefulness had made me wish that other people can also see the radiance I am talking about.*

Mary, Our Lady is already the Queen of Heaven and Earth, but the Devil would also want to have the biggest number of souls it can get. At the end, it is really a battle for souls, salvation or damnation. We can pray for our own and help Our Lady save as many souls as possible.

What was notable about all these was that I started my note-taking as a mystic after my birthday on July 2016. The coronavirus pandemic may have started on December 2019 but the whole year of 2020 was really quite problematic. It had been exactly 42 months or three years and a half, as Our Lady had told me.

What differentiates this pandemic is that there were other things going on too. There were the monstrous hurricanes, the very strong earthquakes, the shaky asteroids and pestilence of locusts in Biblical proportions. It's like everything coming together all at once like a show of force.

Still, thank you. To Jesus through Mary, our Queen of Heaven and Earth!

I wrote then that I did not know when "exactly the 42 months or three years and a half would start." It seems like that officially started in the beginning of 2020. I became a mystic after my 51st birthday in 2016, which would count the 42 months until January 2020, when the global pandemic coronavirus started to spread. It actually began December of 2019. It seems like that was when the fuse was lit.

It seems like "*I saw in my vision like a multitude of angels, like an army size, descending from heaven and helping out living people*" seems credible enough during the pandemic.

"*I do know from my vision that heaven and earth will still exist but the transition between the old and the new world will be very chaotic both with man-made and natural disasters.*" Chaos. There's the man-made chaos such as protesting the death of George Floyd, the Capitol riot, several, several town-based riots. There were also the natural disasters such as record-breaking tornadoes and freezing winter storms.

From the blog Mary Z Rewriting the Faith. Writing # 3

The Unheeded Obligation to Our Lady of Fatima

After visions of angels preparing the three children Lucia and her cousins Jacinta and Francisco, to meet our Lady, her first apparition took place on May 13, 1917 on a Sunday. In 1929, while Lucia was praying in the chapel at Tuy, our Lady appeared to her to ask for the fulfillment of her previous request: "I shall come to ask for the Consecration of Russia to my Immaculate Heart. If they heed my request, Russia will be converted and there will be peace."[66]

Now more than 60 years after Father de Marchi wrote the book about the apparition of Our Lady of Fatima, Our Lady's request for the Consecration of Russia BY NAME to the Immaculate Heart of Mary remains UNHEEDED. Pope John Paul II consecrated the world to Our Lady of Fatima in 1982, 1984, 1991 and 2000, which although brought about much-needed grace, it has not fulfilled the specific request of Our Lady. We hope that the Catholic Church will not forget and keep unheeded our obligation to Our Lady so that our Holy Mother may intercede for peace and prevent the "annihilation of nations" in our behalf.

---

[66] John de Marchi, LMC. "The True Story of Fatima. A Complete Account of Fatima Apparitions." The Fatima Center. New York.

In the past several decades of my own life, Russia had been known to lead the nations to turn away from God and spread the evil of Godlessness. Expert authorities such as Fr. Joaquin Alonso, the official archivist of Fatima, who had talked with Sister Lucy many times, explained that the true conversion of Russia meant not only the return of the Russian people to Orthodox Christian religions. Conversion also meant rejecting the Marxist atheism and most importantly, the total integral conversion of Russia to the one true Church of Christ, the Catholic Church.

Victor Khroul, Director of the Information Center of the Conference of Catholic Bishops of Russia interpreted the "conversion of Russia" as the passing or transformation of non-believers in God, to the Christian faith.

Within that holy hour, I also borrowed an old tattered Bible held together by pieces of scotch tapes. I was browsing it through also looking at the bookmarks previous readers might have left there. My attention was drawn to pages where I don't believe there were any bookmarks but I found it anyway. The Book of Isaiah, Chapters 24 through 29. These chapters pretty much speak of Isaiah's apocalyptic vision. Godlessness is the reason for the chaos and ruin of the world and the only salvation comes from acknowledgment of the One True God and repentance from our evil ways. I just let myself be guided in choosing verses that spoke to me from the Bible.

The Marking of the Fatima's 100th Year

Figuring out the numbers mentioned in the Bible, it looked like one day for God is one year for people. This great "day" of battle between Mary and the serpent, would probably start the year of 2017, where the first apparition of Our Lady of Fatima will have its centennial, and the 100 years given to Satan should end. The year 2017 was marked with a full solar eclipse. 1917 was marked with a miracle of the Sun, while a hundred years later came the full solar eclipse where the Sun's corona was visible.

Photo of 2017 solar eclipse with a red filter.
Photograph by Fernando Felixberto.

And everything stood still as people watched the solar eclipse pass by. From Revelations, the new heaven and earth will have peace for 1000 years. I interpreted this new heaven and earth as a renewed nature of the world where God's will, peace, love and joy reign. After that 1000 years, the Devil will be let out for some time again.

About 33 years later from Pope's vision, Mary's apparition in Fatima, Portugal occurred. It was May, 1917, when three children, Jacinta, 7, Francisco, 9 and Lucia, 10, claimed to have encountered the Virgin Mary on their way home from tending a flock of sheep. The oldest among the three, Lucia, was the only one to speak to her, and Mary told the children, that she would reappear to them on the thirteenth day of the next six months and then vanished. The children soon told their parents. Although some believed the tale, others did not, but the news spread. As the weeks and months passed by, more and more pilgrimages of the faithful were made to Fatima, where the children claimed to receive Mary's visits. Only Lucia could see the apparition of the Virgin Mary and she described her visions to the gathered crowd. To the rest of the crowd, what happened was what called in history, "the miracle of the dancing Sun."

It was Mary's final appearance, on Oct. 13, 1917, that became the most famous. In his book "Looking for a Miracle," Joe Nickell states that "an estimated 70,000 people were in attendance at the site, anticipating the Virgin's final visit and with many fully expecting that she would work a great miracle. As before, the figure appeared, and again only to the children. Identifying herself as 'the Lady of the Rosary,' she urged repentance and the building of a chapel at the site." It was said that after predicting an end to (World War I) and giving the children certain undisclosed visions, the lady lifted her hands to the sky. Thereupon Lucia exclaimed, "The sun!" Everyone gazed upward and saw that a silvery disc had emerged from behind clouds. They experienced what is known (as) a "sun miracle".

Not everyone reported the same thing; some present claimed they saw the sun dance around the heavens; others said the sun zoomed toward Earth in a zigzag motion that caused them to fear that it might collide with our planet (or, more likely, burn it up). Some people reported seeing brilliant colors spin out of the sun in a psychedelic, pinwheel pattern, and thousands of others present didn't see anything unusual at all. The whole event took about 10 minutes, and this Miracle of the Sun, as it became known, is one of the best-known events at Fátima.

The solar eclipse of August 21, 2017 was dubbed as "The Great American Eclipse" by the media. It was a total solar eclipse visible within a band that spanned the entire contiguous United States passing from the Pacific to the Atlantic coasts. As a partial solar eclipse, it was visible on land from Nunavut in Northern Canada to as far south as northern South America. In northwestern Europe and Africa, it was partially visible in the late evening. In Asia, it was only visible at the eastern extremity, the Chukchi Peninsula.

Prior to this event, no solar eclipse had been visible across the entire contiguous United States since June 8, 1918, nine months after the occurrence of the Miracle of the Sun in Fatima, Portugal.

The path of totality touched 14 states, and the rest of the U.S. had a partial eclipse.

The Red October

The La Salette apparition took place in 1846. Pope Leo's vision took place in 1884, with about 4 decades in between. In 1917, about 71 years from the La Salette apparition and 33 years after Pope Leo's prophecy, came Mary's apparition in Fatima, Portugal. Blessed Virgin Mary first appeared to three children, Jacinta, 7, Francisco, 9 and Lucia, 10, on their way home from tending a flock of sheep. The oldest among the three, Lucia was the only one to speak to her, and Mary told the children that she would reappear to them on the thirteenth day of the next six months. The children told their parents. Although some believed the claim, others did not but the news spread anyway. As the weeks and months passed by, the faithful came to do more and more pilgrimages to the site in Fatima, where the children claimed to have received Mary's visits. Only Lucia could see the Virgin Mary's apparition and she described her visions to the gathered crowd. The crowd saw what is now called in history, "the miracle of the dancing Sun." This celestial phenomenon took place on October 13, 1917. Two weeks later, the Red October Revolution took place with which began the Communist persecution of religion in Russia.

The events that took place in 1917, both with the Fatima apparition and the Russian Revolution that began the Communist persecution of the Church offers a logical reasoning behind my intuitive claim that the Miracle of the Sun signified a go-signal for the 100 years test of the Church's survival, as challenged by Satan and allowed by the Lord.

Russia is the largest country in the world by area (6,612,100 sq.mi. or 17,125, 200 sq.km) covering more than one-eighth of the Earth's inhabited land area. Russia's capital Moscow is one of the largest cities in the world. Russia is the ninth most populous country, with over 144 million people as of December, 2017, excluding Crimea. Russia extends across the entirety of Northern Asia and much of Eastern Europe. About 77% of the population live in the western European part of the country. From northwest to southwest, Russia shares land borders with Norway, Finland, Estonia, Latvia, Lithuania, Poland (both with Kaliningrad Oblast), Belarus, Ukraine, Georgia, Azerbaijan, Kazakhstan, China, Mongolia and North Korea. It shares maritime borders with Japan by the Sea of Okhotsk and the US state of Alaska across the Bering Strait.

The Christian community that grew into what was to become the Russian Orthodox Church is traditionally said to have been founded by Christ's apostle Andrew, brother of Simon Peter. Andrew means manly, brave from the Greek word "Andreia" meaning manhood, valor. Andrew, according to the Christian tradition was born in 6 B.C. in the village of Bethsaida in Galilee and known to have lived until the 1st century A.D. Known as Saint Andrew in the Orthodox tradition, he is referred to as the First-Called.

In both the Gospels of Matthew and Mark, the narratives recorded that Jesus walking along the shore of the Sea of Galilee, observed both Simon and Andrew fishing and called them both together to discipleship as "fishers of men." In contrast, in the Gospel of John recalls that Andrew at once recognized Jesus as the Messiah, and introduced him to his brother, Simon. At the beginning of Jesus' public life, they were said to have shared the same house at Capernaum. Andrew was the one who told Jesus about the boy with the loaves and fishes.

Apostle Andrew was thought to have visited Scythia and the Greek colonies along the northern coast of the Black Sea. He was said to have reached the future location of Kiev and foretold the beginnings of a great Christian City. The spot where he reportedly erected a cross is now marked by St. Andrew's Cathedral. The relics of Apostle Andrew are kept at the Basilica of Saint Andrew in Patras, Greece; in Amalfi Cathedral (the Duomo di Sant' Andrea), Amalfi, Italy; St. Mary's Roman Catholic Cathedral, Edinburg, Scotland and the Church of St. Andrew and St. Albert in Warsaw, Poland. Warsaw, the capital city of Poland is about 400 miles away from Wadowice. Wadowice is the birthplace of St. John Paul the Great who was pope from 1978-2005 and has been a recurring theme for me in my interpretations of the Marian prophecies.

In 1914, there were 55,173 Russian Orthodox churches and 29,593 chapels, 112,629 priests and deacons, 500 monasteries and 475 convents with a total of 95,229 monks and nuns in Russia.[67]

In the early March of 1917, the Czar was forced to abdicate. Three months later, the Virgin Mary's first apparition in Fatima, Portugal took place. Within those months, Mary appeared every 13th of the month to the three shepherd children as she had promised. By August 1917, the separation of the Church and State in Russia was forcibly complete. Again, three months after, the Blessed Mother made her final appearance in October, marked with the miracle of the Sun.

In the first five years after the Bolshevik revolution, 28 bishops and 1,200 priests were executed.[68]

During that time when the Russian Orthodox Church fell under persecution of the Communists and the fateful events were taking place, the Blessed Mother Mary spoke through miraculous apparitions.

In 1917, Communist persecution of religion in Russia began.

The year 1917 was a major turning point for the history of Russia and that of the Russian Orthodox Church. The Russian empire was dissolved. The Tsarist government, which had

---

[67] "Russian Orthodox Church" New World Encyclopedia.Retrieved from https://www.newworldencyclopedia.org/entry/Russian_Orthodox_Church#:~:text=In%20the%20first%20five%20years,or%20sent%20to%20labor%20camps. April 6, 2021.

[68] Ibid.

granted the Church numerous privileges was overthrown. The Bolsheviks took power in 1917 after a few months of political turmoil and declared a separation of church and state thereafter.

The Russian Orthodox Church lost its official support from the state for the first time in history. The government seized all church lands. One of the first decrees of the new Communist government, issued in January 1918 declared freedom of "religious and anti-religious propaganda." This led to a marked decline in the power and influence of the Church. The Church was also caught in the crossfire of the Russian Civil War that began later during the same year. The Church supported the White Army that would also turn out to be on the losing side after the October Revolution and resulted into an increased animus from the Bolsheviks. According to Lenin, there was just no place for the Church in Lenin's classless society, therefore, a communist regime cannot remain neutral on the question of religion but be merciless towards it.

Even prior to the end of the Civil War and during the establishment of the Soviet Union, the Russian Orthodox Church came under persecution of the Communist government. The Soviet government espoused militant atheism and viewed the church as a "counter-revolutionary" organization and an independent voice with a great influence in the society. While the Soviet Union officially claimed religious tolerance, in practice, it discouraged organized religion and did everything possible to eradicate its influence from the Soviet society.

The Russian Orthodox Church's support to the previous tsarist Russia was another compelling reason why the Bolsheviks wanted to diminish the Church's influence on the Russian people and government.

Since Pope Leo's vision did not include a specific time setting or time frame, I assumed nobody really knew when that "100 years of test" by Satan actually started. For some reason though,

I thought that the miracle of the Sun in 1917, during the Fatima apparition, must have been the go-signal of this century of test.

From much of my Marian devotion, I know that enmity has been set between the serpent and the Lady. God said: "And I will put enmity between you and the woman, and between your offspring and hers; he will crush your head, and you will strike his heel." (Genesis 3:15) In the image of **Our Lady of the Miraculous Medal,** the Blessed Mother has a serpent under her feet. I pretty much presumed that Satan's challenge had the Blessed Mother as the counterpart.

Everyone alive today should know through some form of history, oral, formal education, media, et cetera, how this past century of two world wars and then some of continuous regional wars, the Great Depression, the recessions, the brutality of rebelling forces, the constant threat of religious extremists or secularist power fanatics and so on and so forth have made the lives of multiple generations pretty difficult. That 100 years that Satan asked to destroy Christ's Church was certainly worth every drop of blood to prove that not even the power of hell, can prevail against the Church, against the people's belief in The One True God.

The Fatima Prophecies

Fatima, 1917

"...In mid-October, Bishop Silva sent her (sister Lucia) a letter containing a direct order to record the secret, and Lucia obeyed.... the third secret was delivered to Silva where it stayed until 1957, when it was finally delivered to Rome. (The third secret) was announced by Cardinal Angelo Sodano on May 13, 2000, 83 years after the first apparition of the Lady to the children in the Cova da Iria, that the Third Secret would finally be released. In his announcement, Cardinal Sodano implied that the secret was about the 20th century persecution of the Christians that culminated in the failed Pope John

Paul II assassination attempt on May 13, 1981, the 64th anniversary of the first apparition of the Lady at Fatima."[69]

I have read Cardinal Sodano's interpretation, which, honestly, sounded like a patchwork of references, something coming from a supposedly logical analysis. Journalists were also not convinced of Sodano's interpretation accusing the Church of hiding part of message. Vatican confirmed that that was the full message. Cardinal Ratzinger, however, whose theological commentary was included in the Congregation's document, essentially said that the Church was still in need of the full meaning of the message.

"After the two parts which I have already explained, at the left of Our Lady and a little above, we saw an Angel with a flaming sword in his left hand; flashing, it gave out flames that looked as though they would set the world on fire; but they died out in contact with the splendour that Our Lady radiated towards him from her right hand: pointing to the earth with his right hand, the Angel cried out in a loud voice: 'Penance, Penance, Penance!' And we saw in an immense light that is God: 'something similar to how people appear in a mirror when they pass in front of it' a Bishop dressed in White 'we had the impression that it was the Holy Father.'"[70]

Sr. Lucia told the interviewers that she was given the vision but not its interpretation. The vision was about the Pope climbing up to the Cross with rough-hewn trunks of cork tree around it, there were corpses or bodies in the wake. The Pope himself was later shot with arrows and more. Reference was also made to "bishops, priests, nuns and lay people." Sr. Lucia said she had the vision but the interpretation belonged to the Church. She was a nun.

In the Fatima message, there was the reference to "there was a white light which was God and then a Bishop in white"

---

[69] "The Message of Fatima" Congregation for the Doctrine of the Faith. Retrieved from https://www.vatican.va/roman_curia/congregations/cfaith/documents/rc_con_cfaith_doc_20000626_message-fatima_en.html. April 6, 2021.

[70] Ibid.

something like a reflection in the mirror." St. Pope John Paul 2 had Sr. Lucia, the visionary at Fatima, sit down with members of the Congregation of the Doctrine of the Faith. She said she did not know which Pope but it was the pope referred to.

Other Bishops, Priests, Religious men and women going up a steep mountain, at the top of which there was a big Cross of rough-hewn trunks as of a cork-tree with the bark; before reaching there the Holy Father passed through a big city half in ruins and half trembling with halting step, afflicted with pain and sorrow, he prayed for the souls of the corpses he met on his way; having reached the top of the mountain, on his knees at the foot of the big Cross he was killed by a group of soldiers who fired bullets and arrows at him, and in the same way there died one after another the other Bishops, Priests, Religious men and women, and various lay people of different ranks and positions. Beneath the two arms of the Cross there were two Angels each with a crystal aspersorium in his hand, in which they gathered up the blood of the Martyrs and with it sprinkled the souls that were making their way to God."[71]

The third secret remains a mystery. None of what happened in St. John Paul II's assassination attempt fit the bill. The world consecration may have been done as Sr. Lucia approved of it which resulted in the demise of Communism in the world. However, the mystique of the Third Secret remains. There is reference to a controversial Pope who dies in the middle of like a raid.

Sr. Lucia also wrote in her memoir, "in Portugal, the dogma will be kept."[72] This refers to Fatima always being remembered in honor of Our Lady's apparition.

---

[71] "The Message of Fatima" Congregation for the Doctrine of the Faith. Retrieved from https://www.vatican.va/roman_curia/congregations/cfaith/documents/rc_con_cfaith_doc_20000626_message-fatima_en.html. April 6, 2021.

[72] "Fatima: A Mystery Explained?" FSSPX News. Retrieved from https://fsspx.news/en/news-events/news/fatima-mystery-explained-41275. April 7, 2021.

Interestingly, in the vision there is reference to a cork tree. It could metaphorically mean that the Church regenerates as the cork tree regenerates. In Aguas de Moura, Palmela, Portugal, there exists the Sobreiro Monumental, also known as the Whistle Tree.[73] It is a 236-year-old cork tree voted European Tree of the Year in 2018. It has been classified as "Tree of Public Interest" since 1988 and is registered in the Guinness Book of Records as "the largest cork oak in the world. It is around 16.2 m (53 ft) tall with a diameter breast height of 4.15m (14 ft.) It was planted between 1783-1784, at that time the Kingdom of Portugal and the Algarves reigned by Queen Maria I and since 1820. Its name "Whistler Tree" comes from the whistling sound of birds that land on its branches. In 1991, the tree yielded over 1,200 kg. (2,646 lb.) of cork, producing more than 100,000 cork stoppers. That would be more than what an average cork tree would produce in its lifetime. In the year 2000, the Sobreiro Monumental was almost cut down together with 411 cork oaks, as an illegal urban expansion took place. By 2001, the law was reformed to better protect the oaks.

Another interesting fact was that Aguas de Moura translates into "water of the woman." I saw in EWTN an episode of the three children of Fatima, where Lucia was dressed like a bride. In another video, it showed the children dressed with like a crown of flowers with a veil behind it. It must have been a silent apocalyptic message, a reference to the Spirit and the Bride. John 16: 12 says, "I have much more to tell you, but now it would be too much for you to bear. When, however, the Spirit comes, who reveals the truth about God, he will lead you into all the truth. He will not speak on his own authority, but he will speak of what he hears and will tell you of things to come." The Spirit in the Bride. The Bride is associated with water. Rev 22:17 says, "The Spirit and the

---

[73] "Sobreiro Monumental" Wikipedia. Retrieved from https://en.wikipedia.org/wiki/Sobreiro_Monumental.
April 7, 2021.

Bride say 'Come! Everyone who hears this must also say 'Come!'
Come, whoever is thirsty; accept the water of life as a gift, whoever
wants it."[74]

My concern with the Third Secret of Fatima is the consistency
about Virgin Mary's concern with the religious. The mountain
referred to in the vision was also mentioned in St. Hildegard von
Bingen.

*After the son of perdition has accomplished all of his evil designs,
he will call together, all of his believers and tell them that he wishes
to ascend to heaven. At the moment of his ascension, a thunderbolt
will strike him into the ground and he will die. The mountain where
he was established for the operation of his ascension, in an instant,
will be covered by a thick cloud which emits an unbearable odor
of truly infernal corruption. At the sight of his body, the eyes of a
great number of persons will open and they will be made to see their
immiserable error. After the sorrowful defeat of the son of perdition,
the spouse of my Son, who is the Church, will shine with the glory
without equal and the victims of error will be impressed to reenter
the sheepfold. As to the day, after the fall of the anti-Christ, when
the world will end, Man must not seek to know for he can never
learn it; that secret the Father has reserved for Himself.*[75]

There were two other visions that I feel have significant
weight. One was about I was talking to Mary and I had a vision of
a dead Pope dressed in like red garments lying in a slab of marble.
I couldn't see who it was then so I asked Mary. I think she might
have answered for me to go ahead check and see. I came closer
and saw that it was Pope John XXIII. This must have been before
that vision when I spoke to him about the vision of the boat, and
his response was, "They will understand." I did not know exactly

---

[74] The Good News Bible. American Bible Society. New York. 1976. p.354.
[75] "We Were Warned: The Prophecies of St. Hildegard von Bingen."
YouTube video by Return to Tradition. December 21, 2018. Retrieved from
https://www.youtube.com/watch?v=MBIRupa9CHc&t=3s. May 5, 2021.

what he meant so I did not say anything back. Pope John XXIII headed out.

Even in my visions, the conversation usually ends with the person I am talking to gesturing that he's leaving the conversation. It's not like they just suddenly disappear into thin air and my vision at that time ends abruptly. I had one insight where I thought about the Council of Trent. The Council of Trent was the Roman Catholic Church's reply to the doctrinal challenges of the Protestant Reformation. It served to define Catholic doctrine and sweeping decrees on self-reform, helping to revitalize the Roman Catholic Church in the face of Protestant expansion. I think at this time, again, there is a challenge to many of the Roman Catholic Church's doctrines, laid out by the Pope Francis papacy. I also thought about the concept of Deus Ex Machina which meant an unexpected power or event that helps to solve or save a seemingly hopeless situation. My mind was running fast-paced. I did not even realize the meaning of Deus Ex Machina until I looked it up. The last time I dealt with it was way back in freshman college which was about some three decades past.

Another vision I was reminded of by the third secret of Fatima with regards to the flaming sword, was while I was at Church praying the Rosary, I must have seen St. Michael first in that particular vision. Then I saw like these knee-high flames and I walked through the flames simply unharmed.

What could be noted from among this particular series of Marian prophecies I am discussing is that there is what can be interpreted as "passing of the torchlight" from among Mary's visionaries. Since human life's term is limited, visionaries seem to carry on the message from one apparition to another in these specific circumstances. I am the one, however, who can weave the whole picture together but the complete information becomes available when the Blessed Mother wants it to be.

The other thing that bothered me quite a lot and was brought again to my attention was during the centennial of the Fatima celebration, I could not understand why in Pope Francis' prayers, he said that he was a "prophet and a messenger." My concern was the word "prophet." I honestly don't believe words from a Pope should be taken too lightly, especially in a very special event celebration, such as the Fatima centennial and the whole world was watching. What prophecy was he referring to? Or does it mean he's claiming he has a prophetic vision. Is he claiming a vision for the Church? However, to me, a prophet is defined as someone who has direct verbal instructions from God to deliver a message, not merely inspired by the Holy Spirit, but real, direct instructions as the prophets from the Old Testament. Having some sense of what is to come, especially if it is intentional, does not necessarily make one a "prophet." A prophet brings direct messages from God, usually have visions about those messages, writes them down or verbalizes them, and then conveys those words directly to the people. So that claim of being a "prophet" bothered me coming from a pope, who should really be quite distinct and most careful with communication.

CHAPTER 17

St. John Paul 2: A Shared Pain

With the image of St. John Paul 2 from the St. John Paul 2 Center in Washington, DC, 2019.

I am talking about St. John Paul 2 as we had some unknown, remote connection. The timing may be a bit different but the connection was there.

On May 13, 1981, Pope John Paul II was supposed to address an audience at St. Peter's Square. It was an anniversary date of Our Lady of Fatima. As he entered St. Peter's Square, he was shot and critically wounded by Mehmet Ali Aqca, a Turkish gunman who was a member of the militant fascist group, Grey Wolves. The assassin used a Browning 9 mm semi-automatic pistol, shooting the pope in the abdomen which perforated John Paul 2's colon and small intestines multiple times. John Paul II was rushed into the Vatican complex and then to the Gemelli Hospital. He lost consciousness on the way to the hospital. Even though the two bullets missed his mesenteric artery and abdominal aorta, he lost nearly three-quarters of his blood and had to go through five hours of surgery to treat his wounds. Surgeons performed a colostomy, temporarily rerouting the upper part of the large intestine to let the damaged lower part heal. When he briefly regained consciousness before the surgery, he instructed the doctors not to remove the Brown Scapular during the operation.

I believe I was around nine or ten years old when Mama gave me the Brown Scapular. It would have been around 1974 or 1975. I never took it off even while taking a bath, because the scapular was laminated and the necklace part was just a thread. I was a pretty happy kid but after a little while I became sickly and lethargic with the scapular. I had recurrent fevers. I looked tired and without energy. I would get better and then I would get sick again. I think it was about two or three times. It seemed like I shared this pain of St. John Paul 2 wearing the Brown Scapular.

Just as I got sick about two more times, there were two other attempts on Pope John Paul II's life. Just a day before the anniversary of the first attempt of life, on May 12, 1982, a man tried to stab him with a bayonet, in Fatima, Portugal. He was injured but survived with a non-critical wound. The third attempt on his life was when a suicide bomber planned to dress as a priest and detonate a bomb as the Pope's motorcade passed by during a 1995 World Youth Day celebration in the Philippines. An inadvertent chemical fire alerted the police to the criminal's whereabouts and all were arrested a week before the pope's visit and confessed to the plot.

After a time of my struggling with health, Mama finally decided it was time to remove the brown scapular of Our Lady of Mt. Carmel from me. I think it was after that, that she introduced me to the novena of Our Lady of Miraculous Medal.

Three days after, as John Paul 2 recovered from the emergency, he told one of his closest friends who was allowed to visit him, philosopher Anna-Teresa Tymienecka that Our Lady of Fatima helped keep him alive throughout his ordeal. *"In everything that happened to me on that very day, I felt that extraordinary motherly protection and care, which turned out to be stronger than the deadly bullet."*[76]

Agca was caught by and restrained by a nun and other bystanders until the police arrived. He was sentenced to life imprisonment. Two days after Christmas in 1983, Pope John Paul II visited him and prison and spoke privately with him for about twenty minutes. He later then said *"I spoke to him as a brother whom I have pardoned and who has my complete trust."*[77] It was said that Aqca never requested to be pardoned but John Paul 2 pardoned him anyway. Aqca was more curious about Our Lady of Fatima who was given credit that John Paul 2 would survive the ordeal. It was said that he was more concerned about the technicality of the shooting and not the morality of it. "Tell me something about this mystery of Fatima because if I understand it correctly, then I can find out why I wasn't able to kill the Pope."[78]

---

[76] "Pope John Paul II" Retrieved from Wikipedia. https://en.wikipedia.org/wiki/Pope_John_Paul_II. April 6, 2021.

[77] Ibid.

[78] "30th Anniversary of John Paul II's Assassination Attempt" Retrieved from YouTube Rome Reports.com, April 9, 2021.

CHAPTER 18

Our Lady of Akita

The message from Our Lady of Akita was not necessarily given to me but I thought since it carries the same message, I will include it here.

Our Lady of Akita is the Catholic title of the Blessed Virgin Mary associated with a wooden statue venerated by faithful Japanese who consider it to be miraculous. The image is popular because of the Marian apparitions reported in 1973 by Sister Agnes Katsuko Sasagawa in the remote area of Yuzawadai, an outskirt of Akita, Japan. The messages emphasize prayer, like the Fatima, frequent recitation of the Holy Rosary and penance. Sasagawa had cryptic visions prophesying sacerdotal persecution and heresy within the Catholic Church.

The apparitions were extraordinary in the sense that the weeping statue of the Virgin Mary was broadcast on Japanese national television and gained further attention with the sudden healing of hearing impairment experienced by Sasagawa after the apparitions. The image also became affiliated with The Lady of All Nations movement with which the message shares some similarities.

It was actually pretty interesting to note that I became a member of the Legion of Mary under the Our Lady of All Nations banner back at St. Louis Church. It was around 2013 through 2016.

Our Lady of All Nations

I moved to Alexandria, Virginia from Wareham, Massachusetts in February of 2013. I noticed there was a parish bulletin in the cracks of my brother's couch. It was St. Louis Church. A few years back, I walked into a church that I am not familiar with but I usually pass by and sat myself in the middle of the Church. I was glad nobody knew me coming from a tradition of serving as a Mass lector, where I almost knew everybody and it was starting to feel more like a job. In the middle of the Church, I told God I was seeking Him. I believe the priest was doing a homily about pro-life versus pro-choice. One of the first things I did then was to talk to a priest, through a confession, saying that I am "thirsty" for God. The priest said he liked my words and suggested that I attend the Church.

I started attending the Masses but I was not really interested in joining any parish organizations. I just wasn't that type.

After the awkward way that I started with the Legion of Mary Our Lady of All Nations praesidium, which I recalled earlier in the book, the assignment of bringing the statue of the Virgin Mary to homes ended up in my lap. I started asking parishioners around after Mass and I started realizing 9 out of 10 people were very eager to have the statue of the Virgin Mary brought to their home. I started compiling a waiting list and shared about half of them, around 55, to the other Legion praesidium. We also had recruitment sessions and started recruiting more people that the praesidium had to split into two because there's too many people in one and the meetings are limited up to only an hour and a half. I would say that would be a pretty successful turn-around.

Usually there's a reason why people invite us to their homes but in setting up the appointments, sometimes some people would take precedence over the others and I would learn from the people themselves why. It may be someone is sick, or someone needs prayers for family concerns, etc. Some of my friends thought that the Virgin Mary was actually using me for the Legion tasks.

There was a time when there was a parish activity and I can almost stand behind the parish priest and greet the parishioners as I have become familiar with almost each of them.

Going back to Our Lady of Akita, the local ordinary of the convent, John Shojiro Ito, Bishop of Niigata (1962-1985) acknowledged the "supernatural character of a series of mysterious events concerning the statue of the Holy Mother Mary" and authorized "the veneration of the Holy Mother of Akita within the Roman Catholic Diocese of Niigata in a 1984 pastoral letter.

Sister Agnes Sasagawa

Sister Agnes Sasagawa was originally from a Buddhist family. She had encountered many health problems for several decades. She was born premature and suffered poor health most of her life. She also had a poorly performed appendectomy and she was immobile for over a decade. Her health was said to have improved after drinking water from Lourdes while she was under the care of a Catholic nun. After going totally deaf, she came to live with the nuns near Akita. In 1973, Sasagawa noted apparitions, as well as stigmata and a wooden statue of the Virgin Mary reported to have wept on 101 occasions. The nuns at Yuzawadai also reported stigmata on the statue as well as on the hands of Sasagawa; the stigmata on the statue reportedly to have appeared before the tears started and disappeared after the tears.

Sasagawa reported three messages from the Blessed Virgin during 1973, the statue however was itself reported to have continued weeping thereafter. Sasagawa indicated that she first heard the statue calling her, and then the first message began.

Sasagawa said that she started receiving the first of the messages from the Virgin Mary on July 6, 1973. Sasagawa described that when this occurred, the statue became illuminated as it acknowledged her stigmata and hearing impairment. The Virgin Mary had instructed her to recite the prayer of the Handmaids of the Eucharist which would cure Sr. Sasagawa's deafness. The other indicated messages ask for the praying of the rosary and to pray Acts of Reparation.

The second message states that "many men in this world afflict the Lord. I desire souls to console Him to soften the anger of the Heavenly Father. I wish, with my Son, for souls who will repair by their suffering and their poverty for the sinners and ingrates."[79]

The third message was given on October 13, 1973. It was said that the statue became animated for an extended time and was witnessed by a number of nuns. The third message from Our Lady of Akita is:

"My dear daughter, listen well to what I have to say to you... As I told you, if men do not repent and better themselves, the Father will inflict a terrible punishment on all humanity. It will be a punishment greater than the deluge, such as one will never have seen before. Fire will fall from the sky and will wipe out a great part of humanity... the good as well as the bad, sparing neither priests nor faithful. The survivors will find themselves so desolate that they will envy the dead... Each day recite the prayer of the rosary. With the rosary pray for the Pope, bishops and the priests. The work of the devil will infiltrate even into the Church in such a way that one will see cardinals opposing cardinals, and bishops against other bishops. The priests who venerate me will be scorned and opposed by their confreres... churches and altars sacked; the Church will be full of those who accept compromises and the demon will press many priests and consecrated souls to leave the service of the Lord. The demon will be especially implacable against souls consecrated to God. The thought of the loss of so many souls is the cause of my sadness. If sins increase in number and gravity, there will be no longer pardon for them. With courage, speak to your superior... It is Bishop Ito, who directs your community. You have

---

[79] "Our Lady of Akita." Retrieved from Wikipedia. https://en.wikipedia.org/wiki/Our_Lady_of_Akita. April 19, 2021.

still something to ask? Today is the last time that I will speak to you in living voice. From now on you will obey the one sent to you and your superior... I alone am able still to save you from the calamities which approach.[80]

Sasagawa had been admitted to the community of the Sisters of Junshin in Nagasaki. She experienced hearing loss in her left ear years earlier while she experienced hearing loss in her right ear for the first time in March 1973 at Myoko, Niigata. On May 12, 1973, Sasagawa moved into the convent of the Seitai Hoshikai Handmaids of the Holy Eucharist at Yuzawadai. The three messages from the statue were perceived by her deaf ears while she was a novice at the convent.

In October 1974, Sasagawa felt a sudden improvement in hearing. In March 1975, Sasagawa began to encounter "violent headaches" and sudden hearing loss. She underwent two hearing examinations in March 1975, the diagnoses of which was hearing loss in both ears. Dr. Sawada of the Niigata Rosai Hospital at Joetsu, Niigata, certified that she was "incurably deaf" and issued some documents for her to receive a state subsidy. Another doctor, Dr. Arai of the Eye and Ear Division of the Akita Red Cross Hospital also confirmed her complete deafness.

In May 1982, Sasagawa suddenly felt that her hearing improved. In June 1982, Dr. Sawada confirmed that Sasagawa's hearing was fully restored, although it was not attested as a "miraculous cure" by the hospital.

On August 4, 1981, a Korean woman with a terminal brain tumor was miraculously healed after friends and relatives prayed for the intercession of Our Lady of Akita. Her name is Teresa Chun Sun Ho. While comatose, she received visions of Mary related to the Akita events during her recovery. Her disease was diagnosed and the subsequent cure was confirmed by medical

---

[80] "Our Lady of Akita." Retrieved from Wikipedia. https://en.wikipedia.org/wiki/Our_Lady_of_Akita. April 19, 2021.

professionals in South Korea. According to Chun and other October 1983 Korean pilgrims, Chun's cure had been declared miraculous by Church authorities of Korea."

With regards to the stigmata, Sasagawa claimed to have had a stigmatic-like experience. His left hand developed bleeding marks. In her left came about bleeding marks. Yasuda wrote that in June 1973, "in the center of (Sasagawa's) palm, were two red scratches in the form of a cross." It seemed to have "been engraved in the skin" and started to bleed a few days later. According to another nun, "there were two red traces in the form of a cross that seemed to cause (Sasagawa) pain. According to Sasagawa's account, the stigmata appeared after she began seeing supernatural beings, which were disclosed to be angels, and two incidents where she experienced piercing pain in the palm of her hand. On the statue, one nun characterized it as a liquid from two intersecting lines described as a "blackish mark." Two other nuns said "it had been traced with a fine point of a pencil" or "traced by a pen with a black ink." A third nun, who was the sacristan, described what she saw as "a wound in the form of a cross, in the middle of the palm of the right hand, cut with something like a tip of a blade." There were several explanations proposed, including the theory of ectoplasmic capability, when the wound appeared on Sasagawa's hand. To theologians though, the stigmata on Sasagawa and the statue's hands were meant as signs.

In December 1973, TV Tokyo Channel 12 videotaped the weeping statue. The blood type of the statue was found to be Type B while its sweat and tear type were found to be Type AB.

CHAPTER 19

Garabandal: Where the Eucharist Belongs

Garabandal, 1961-1965

The message which Our Lady has given the world through the intercession of St. Michael the Archangel. The angel said, "Since my message of October 18 has not been made known to the world and has not been fulfilled. I tell you that this is my last message. Previously, the cup was being filled. Now it is overflowing. Many Cardinals, many Bishops and many priests are on the road to perdition and with them they are bringing many souls. The Holy Eucharist is being given less importance (honor)."[81]

---

[81] "Four Messages from Our Lady of Garabandal" Garabandal.org. Retrieved from http://www.garabandal.org/News/Message_7.shtml. April 6, 2021.

The Brown Scapular

The *Brown Scapular* that Pope John Paul II asked the doctors not to remove links us to the Garabandal prophecies. On July 2, 1961, Mary appeared as Our Lady of Mount Carmel also bearing a brown scapular. This scapular is the habit of both the Carmelite Order and the Discalced Carmelite Order that has served as the prototype of other devotional scapulars. According to the Vatican's Congregation for Divine Worship, it is "an external sign of the filial relationship established between Mary and the faithful who entrust themselves totally to her protection.

Our Lady appeared to the four girls on July 2, 1961 accompanied by two angels, one being St. Michael. The girls described their vision as follows:

> *"She is dressed in a white robe with a blue mantle and a crown of golden stars. Her hands are slender. There is a brown scapular on her right arm, except when she carried the Child Jesus in her arms. Her hair, deep nut-brown, is parted in the center. Her face is long, with a fine nose. Her mouth is very pretty with lips a bit thin. She looks like a girl of eighteen. She is rather tall. There is no voice like hers. No woman just is just like her, either in*

the voice or the face or anything else. Our Lady manifested herself as Our Lady of Carmel."[82]

"Before all that arrives, great disorders will arrive in the Church and everywhere. Then, after (that) our Holy Father, the Pope will be persecuted (from all sides, they will shoot at him, they will want to put him to death, but no one will be able to do it, the Vicar of God will triumph again this time.) His successor will be a pontiff that nobody expects.

Then after (that) a great peace, will come, but it will not last a long time. A monster will come to disturb it. All that I tell you here will arrive in the other century, at the latest in the year two thousand."[83]

Following the death of Pope John Paul II in 2005, Joseph Aloisius Ratzinger became Pope Benedict XVI and served in the Vatican from 2005 to 2013. Time magazine quoted unnamed sources saying that Ratzinger was a front runner candidate to succeed John Paul II should he die or become too ill to continue as pope. Before his election as pope, Ratzinger was considered to be one of 100 most influential people in the world by Time magazine. Ratzinger was "a major figure in the Vatican for a quarter of a century"[84] and he was seen as having clout second to none when it came to setting church priorities and directions as one of John Paul II's closest confidants. He has lived in Rome since 1981. What was more surprising of Pope Benedict XVI was that on February 11, 2013, he announced his resignation citing a "lack of strength in mind and body" due to his

---

[82] "The Beginning". The Garabandal Story. Retrieved from http://www.garabandal.org/story.shtml May 5, 2021.

[83] Ibid.

[84] "Pope Benedict XVI. Wikipedia. Retrieved from https://en.wikipedia.org/wiki/Pope_Benedict_XVI. May 5, 2021.

advanced age. He was the first pope to resign since Pope Gregory XII in 1415 and the first to do so on his own initiative since Pope Celestine V in 1294. His resignation became effective on February 28, 2013 with the title of pope emeritus.

The pope who actually defied expectations was an Argentinian Cardinal Jorge Mario Bergoglio who took on the name of Pope Francis. Francis is the first Jesuit pope, the first from the Americas, the first from the Southern Hemisphere and the first pope from outside Europe since the Syrian Gregory III who reigned in the 8th century. He is the current Bishop of Rome.

The Warning

"On May 2, 1962, the angel told Conchita that God would perform a miracle so that all people would believe: they would see the Sacred Host on her tongue at the moment of Communion and that she should make this known fifteen days in advance. On July 18, 1962, the town was crowded with visitors. At midnight Conchita, who had remained in her home continually surrounded by visitors, entered into ecstasy and went out into the street. At a short distance from her house, she fell down on her knees in the midst of the crowd. Lanterns were focused on her. She put out her tongue upon which nothing was resting, as everyone could see. In a few moments, a white host appeared on her tongue and remained there for a few minutes. A businessman from Barcelona, Don Alejandro Damians, standing less than three feet from the girl, secured some very good moving pictures. In the film there appeared 79 pictures of the extraordinary scene. This same witness wrote a report which he submitted to the Bishop of Santander, together with a copy of the film."[85]

"Since my message of October 18, 1961 has not been complied with and has not been made much known to the world, I will tell

---

[85] "Four Messages from Our Lady of Garabandal" Garabandal.org. Retrieved from http://www.garabandal.org/News/Message_7.shtml. April 6, 2021.

you that this is the last one. Before the chalice was filling now it is overflowing. Many Cardinals, many Bishops and many priests are on the path to perdition and they take many souls with them. To the Eucharist, there is given less and less importance. We should avoid the wrath of God on us by our good efforts. If you ask pardon with your sincere soul God will pardon you. It is I, your Mother, who through the intercession of St. Michael, wish to say that you amend, that you are already in the last warnings and that I love you much and do not want your condemnation. Ask us sincerely and we will give to you. You should sacrifice more. Think of the Passion of Jesus.

Tuesday (June 19, 1962) Loli and I were in the Calleja (place near the first apparition) and she (The Virgin) told us a message for the whole world and it is this: the Virgin has said to us that we are not awaiting the chastisement because we are disregarding her first message by the way we live but without awaiting it, it will come because the world has not changed and now with this (Message). She has said it twice and we do not heed her because the world is worse and must change much but has not changed at all. Prepare yourselves Confess for the Chastisement will come soon. The world continues the same and I think that the world has not changed at all. What a pity that it does not change. Soon the Great Chastisement will come if it (the world) does not change. This message was given to Loli and me."

Conchita wrote: "The warning comes directly from God and will be visible to the whole world and from any place where anyone may happen to be. It will be like the revelation of our sins and it will be seen and felt by everyone, believer and unbeliever alike irrespective of whatever religion he may belong to. It will be seen and felt in all parts of the world and by every person."

"It will happen in the sky, no one can prevent it from happening....than to pass through this Warning. It will not kill us. It will be a "correction" of our conscience. It will cause great fear and will make us reflect within ourselves on the consequences of our own personal sins. It will be like a warning of the punishment to come. In this way the world will be offered a means of purification to prepare itself for the extraordinary grace of the Great Miracle.

Jacinta was told by Our Blessed Mother "that the warning would come when conditions were at their worst." This date was not revealed to the visionaries, however Mari-Loli does know the year, and she said that "the miracle will happen one year after the warning."

The solar eclipse of August 21, 2017, dubbed the "Great American Eclipse"[86] by the media, was a total solar eclipse visible within a band. It spanned the contiguous United States from the Pacific to the Atlantic coasts. It was also visible as a partial solar eclipse from as far north as Nunavut in northern Canada to as far south as northern South America. In northwestern Europe and Africa, it was partially visible in the late evening. In northeastern Asia, it was partially visible at sunrise.

Prior to this event, no solar eclipse had been visible across the entirety of the United States since June 8, 1918 and not since the February 1979 eclipse had a total eclipse been visible from anywhere in the mainland United States. The path of totality touched 14 states, and the rest of the U.S. had a partial eclipse. The area of the path of totality was about 16 percent of the area of the United States, with most of this area over the ocean, not land.

I myself experienced the event. Slowly, the eclipse rolled out state-by-state. It would be like about 10 to 15 minutes and the next phase would be seen in another state. It was kind of like how coronavirus rolled out in the contiguous United States two years later. "It will be like a warning of the punishment to come. In this way the world will be offered a means of purification to prepare itself for the extraordinary grace of the Great Miracle."

"In this way the world will be offered a means of purification to prepare itself for the extraordinary grace of the Great Miracle. The Miracle will happen within one year after The Warning."

---

[86] "Solar eclipse of August 21, 2017" Wikipedia. Retrieved from https://en.wikipedia.org/wiki/Solar_eclipse_of_August_21,_2017. May 21, 2021.

I am still in question though of the Great Miracle to "happen within one year after the Warning. Unless, I think, this is the Great Miracle occurring now. The connections between Mary's prophecies and its impact on the Church. There have been several implicit guides for me: Mary's icons, St. Pope John Paul II, my own mystical visions and conversations with Mary and my life experiences such as travel to the places or attendance to certain events, all leading to that thematic message within the prophecies. The Garabandal apparition, through its visionaries offers more details about the issues within the Church. Mary's focus from all these visions have been about the Catholic Church and St. Pope John Paul 2 as the common thread.

The other Great Miracle undeniably is my mystic gift. I have been a mystic since I was a child beginning since I have become aware at seven years old. Or should I say blessed with extra sensory perception. It runs in the family though although my mystic gift have taken a far wider and larger context. I will have had to learn about my abilities and purpose. Mama seems to have prepared me especially for the purpose of my gift.

Before the pandemic coronavirus happened, I have given predictions about it. I saw this painting of like orange flowers, more like orange balls hanging at my doctor's office. I emailed about it and warned that it will be like "dominoes one falling after another." It occurred to me that I was essentially talking about countries being plagued one after the other with the coronavirus.

The second time I remember talking about this was that I was responding to some email and I said something like "everybody will be walking this time."

And the third time, I talked about it was I referring to New York, like something happened, like a bomb hit New York. I couldn't figure out then exactly what I was talking about, in terms of gravity or immensity. New York at one point became the epicenter of the coronavirus. I believe it was around 2019 that I talked about New York. I must have been talking about the "dominoes" back in 2017 and "everybody walking" must have been 2018. I could sense that something big was going to happen, I just did not have a concrete idea of how it will take place. Things become much clearer after everything had occurred.

Our Lady of Guadalupe and St. Lucy

The essence of my writing today, Christmas Eve, was that, last July 23rd, five days prior to my birthday, this year, I wrote some notes about the Fatima and the Garabandal Marian messages.

"In Garabandal, there was a mention about a saint who has a Eucharistic significance and a Thursday feast day. There's two this year, St. Gregory and St. Lucy. Like anything else, I had to refer to my personal experiences to decipher the meanings. I realized when I got to attend the feast day celebration of St. Lucy in Italy, there was a bright light reflected from what would have been the stained-glass window. I did not see the window from where I was standing at. I just presumed. The reflection looked like a human figure particularly. On a closer look, it looked like it was floating in the air, very colorful. St. Lucy's feast day is on December 13. She has Eucharistic significance in terms of where the "Sanctus" is put in the Mass.

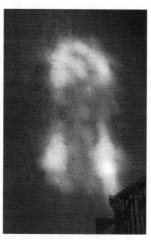

*An image on the wall at the Church of
St. Lucy, Sicily, Italy, 2004.*

On December 13, 2018, when I come close to the image of Our Lady of Guadalupe, there shines with me like an aura of white light. The pastor then was talking about St. Lucy in his baptismal homily and I remembered my notes where I linked St. Lucy and Our Lady of Guadalupe.

Our Lady of Guadalupe, 2018. *With Our Lady of Guadalupe, 2018.*

CHAPTER 20

At the St. John Paul 2 Center

I once, on occasion, got to visit the St. John Paul 2 Center in Washington DC. The camera seems to capture the electricity I bring into the room.

The altar at the main chapel, St. John Paul 2 Center, Washington DC, 2019.

With the altar as the background, at the Main Chapel, St. John Paul 2 Center, 2019.

*Our Lady of
Guadalupe, 2019.*

*With the image of Our
Lady of Guadalupe.*

CHAPTER 21

Corpus Christi Sunday, 2019

*During the Corpus Christi Sunday, At St. Anthony
de Padua Church, Falls Church, Virginia, 2019.*

It was two Sundays ago, June 23, 2019, Corpus Christi Sunday
was a huge miracle for me. A couple of Sundays before that and
even then, I thought that it was magical that the sunlight from
the Skylight ceiling windows would light up simultaneous with
specific parts of the Mass or specific lines recited. I have to pull
up my notes on these later. During this Corpus Christi Sunday, I

was actually running behind schedule. I got to the Church later than my normal time and somebody had already taken the spot where I usually sit at. I sat on the left side of that pew. It must have been around the Consecration time that the Sun shone so strongly on me, on my face. I had to cover my eyes to see what the priest was doing. I looked around and the sunlight seemed more liked a spotlight directed on me in the whole Church! The only other spot was on the other side of the pew but it was much smaller. It fell on an elderly lady's hand as she was praying.

When I kneeled down, I thought, when I stand up then I won't have much of the light but actually it was the same if not more. All that time during the Consecration and Communion, it felt like I was bathed in sunlight that everything around me was darker. I could still see the people but it was rather darker. I just prayed then sometimes with my face in my hands. I was actually praying to God, saying, "Daddy!!!!" because He had like the spotlight on me!!! I also thought and prayed however about "my Church!!!" I was telling Daddy. "my Church!!!" After I received the Holy Communion, I just prayed. I usually look at the people around me but since I could hardly see much with the bright light on me and everything around me was darker, I just prayed with my face in my hands. I believe everyone saw the light shining on me directly. It was nowhere else in the whole Church. I was saying, "Daddy!!!!!!"

Briefly, I said, "My Church!!!!!" Corpus Christi Sunday!!! Everyone had a brief moment of pause. After the Mass, the pastor came up to the front, first to give thanks to the priest who was leaving the parish then for another assignment. He then gave instructions on how the procession will proceed. I did see him smile at me even through that dark ambiance. I was at the corner of the pew almost directly across the pulpit at the altar

After the congregation stood up from the pews to follow the Eucharistic procession, I looked back on the spot where I was and there was indeed a ray of sunshine on my spot.

When the congregation came back from the procession, a milder sunshine was there where a young woman was, but it didn't have that ray of light effect. The sunshine shone more brightly at the altar, and the monstrance and the crucifix on the altar. It looked like shining white!!!

I actually looked back. I saw that there was like a ray of sunshine right straight to where I was.

I remembered that because when the crowd got back to the Church, the Sun still shone through the skylights window but without the direct ray of sunshine.

But the Sunlight was now then on the Eucharist at the altar. I took a picture because the monstrance was shining bright.

I'm going to attach some pictures. See the monstrance. It's practically white. The altar candle in front of the Tabernacle was like at a perfect angle from where I was. I just noticed that now since I was looking at the monstrance.

PART 2

Saintly Prophecies about the Anti-Christ

After the occurrence of Christ's Transfiguration, Peter offered to build three tents for Jesus, Moses and Elijah. When Peter looked up, there was only Jesus and His response was "Get behind me, Satan!" Jesus' reply seemed irrational, almost cruel. There were several interpretations why Jesus would have rebuffed Peter with, "Get behind me, Satan." Jesus was actually foretelling the problem that would plague His Church. The papal abuse and the papal misdeeds. Until such time of Jesus' promised to come back, and still throughout, the Blessed Mother Mary had been accompanying the journey of her Son's Church. She had appeared in various apparitions, which some trackers recorded 386 sightings[87], in the 20th century alone, 299 of which, the Vatican had not officially commented upon. The Vatican does not comment about the supernatural character of most of them.

---

[87] Apparitions Statistics, Modern. Marian Apparitions of the 20th and 21st Centuries. A Directory of 20th and 21st century Apparition through 2011. University of Dayton. Retrieved from https://udayton.edu/imri/mary/a/apparitions-statistics-modern.php#:~:text=A%20statistical%20analysis%20of%20the,299%20of%20the%20386%20cases. May 17, 2021.

"Tales of gays in the Vatican have been told for more than a thousand years. Pope John XII, who reigned from 955 to 964, was accused of having sex with men and boys and turning the papal palace into a whorehouse. While trying to persuade a cobbler's apprentice to have sex with him, Pope Boniface VIII, who reigned from 1294 to 1303 was said to have assured the boy that two men having sex was "no more a sin than rubbing your hands together.[88]

After Paul II, who reigned from 1464 to 1471, died of a heart attack – while in **flagrante delicto** *with a page, according to one rumor – he was succeeded by Sixtus IV, who kept a nephew as his lover (and made the nephew a cardinal at age 17). Some such stories are better substantiated than others. Even while their reliability is questionable, they demonstrate that playing the gay card (even if you yourself are gay) is an ancient Curial tactic.[89]*

According to Mark D. Jordan, author of *The Silence of Sodom: Homosexuality in Modern Catholicism*, there are closeted gay priests who are vipers. *"They are really poisonous people, and they work out their inner demonology by getting into positions in power and exercising it against other gay men, women and anyone whom they perceive to be a threat. Alongside that are suffering priests who seem sincere all the way down who are trying to be faithful to God, and also to take care of people and change the institution. They are the ones who are always forgotten and read out of the story from both sides.[90]"*

The day was when the Supreme Court will vote for or against same-sex marriage. I was at the office. I decided to come by the front desk as if I have been summoned but I was only going to check if there were any mail that had come in. While I was at the front

---

[88] Gross, Michael Joseph. "The Vatican's Secret Life" December 2013. Vanity Fair. Retrieved from https://www.vanityfair.com/culture/2013/12/gay-clergy-catholic-church-vatican. May 17, 2021.

[89] Gross, Michael Joseph. "The Vatican's Secret Life" December 2013. Vanity Fair. Retrieved from https://www.vanityfair.com/culture/2013/12/gay-clergy-catholic-church-vatican. May 17, 2021.

[90] Ibid.

desk, I saw people on TV celebrating, some were being interviewed. The same-sex marriage had been approved. I stood there for a few moments, like frozen, like I have turned into a rock of salt. "How could this be?" I asked. I was fearful of what might happen then.

The problem with the Catholic Church primarily, among other things, is the corrupting presence of homosexuality that had given way to depraved immoral acts. The consistent theme of these four apparitions of Mary is one of an intense, sorrowful but special concern especially for the religious members of the Church who have lost their way particularly because of the presence and challenge of Satan from within. It is a special concern for their souls manifested in a collaborative divine and human way to offer relief and redemption.

Marian apparitions should be interpreted as both in a progressive continuum of particular events but also as something concurrent. The process of time cannot be understood in merely a human way. Although the Marian apparitions have occurred decades or centuries apart, the transcendent consistency and value or meaning is there.

The bigger context also needs to be understood. This is also the millennium when the Blessed Mother's role in salvation history had been much presented.

To me, a stunning part of the revelations of the Marian messages is that it coincides to many things that Mama had mentioned to me or taught me. It was pretty difficult not to be in awe or be in a huge surprise that things that were too mundane seemed to connect with me in a very personal way. I have also noticed that St. John Paul 2 the Great is a connecting theme from the apparitions.

What does the Catholic Church say regarding prophecies?

To start on the right footing, it is best to know ourselves with what the Church has to say about this topic. For our enlightenment, let us refer to the Catholic Encyclopedia for some guidelines regarding prophecies. To quote it verbatim:

"As the term prophecy is used in mystical theology, it also applies to both the prophecies of canonical Scripture and to private prophecies.

In its strict sense, prophecy is understood as the foreknowledge of future events, though sometimes it may apply to events of which there is no past memory, and to present hidden things which cannot be known by the natural light of reason.

According to St. Paul, speaking of prophecy in 1 Corinthians 14, prophecy does not limit its meaning to prediction of future events. Prophecies, include rather, divine inspirations concerning what is secret, whether future or not. As the manifestation of hidden present mysteries or past events comes under revelation, we have to understand the strictest and most proper sense of prophecy, namely the revelation of future events.

The knowledge of the prophecy must be supernatural and infused by God because it concerns things beyond the natural power of created intelligence, the knowledge must be supernatural and because the gift of prophecy is given primarily for the good of others, it must be manifested either by words or signs.

It is a divine light by which God reveals things concerning the unknown future and by which these things are in some way represented to the mind of the prophet, whose duty it is to manifest them to others.

The Church regards the Apocalypse as divinely inspired and remains to be the last prophetic work. It is acknowledged as such. Though the prophetic spirit remained throughout the centuries, the Church has never promoted any other prophetic work even as she proclaimed countless saints who were gifted with prophecy. The Church prudently gives plenty of latitude as to the acceptance or rejection of particular or private prophecies based on evidence for or against them. The Catholic faithful's attitude should be that of prudence and balance, always being careful and slow in accepting or rejecting them especially when they come from trustworthy sources and do not contradict Catholic doctrine or morals.

The veracity or accuracy of the fulfillment of these prophecies remains to be the litmus test to which all of them will be judged. The character of these prophecies covers a pretty wide scope ranging from pious anticipations of Providence; to events in the lives of saints; to the fate of nations; to the popes and the papacy; and to apocalyptic catastrophes leading to the end of the world. They may sometimes be realized in part and in part may even run contrary to events. Due to the conditional essence of some of them, they may or may not be fulfilled, or some fulfilled in one form or another."[91]

The prophecies will be discussed in more details later in the book.

There have been saints prior to myself who have had visions about the anti-Christ. I only took the major ones: St. Malachy, St. Hildegard, St. Anna Katherine of Emmerich and St. Francis of Assisi. The others talked about a darkness to come but did not talk about the anti-Christ specifically. These were Blessed Anna of Taigi, St. Columbkille and St. Bernadette of Sweden.

The way I came across St. Malachy was that I was reading one of the books I ordered online about Mary Magdalene. There was a little phrase in the middle of the book about "De labore solis" and St. John Paul 2. I thought I remembered Dr. Taylor Marshall, an online evangelist, having some video presentations about St. Malachy so I immediately got up and check it out.

I still would want to leave plenty of the prophetic verses open to interpretation and dwell onto a few significant others.

---

[91] "Prophecy." Catholic.com. Retrieved from https://www.catholic.com/encyclopedia/prophecy. May 17, 2021.

CHAPTER 22

St. Malachy

Attributed to St. Malachy is "Prophecy of the Popes" wherein he claims there will only be 112 more popes before the Last Judgment. Benedict Arnold de Wyon discovered and published the so-called "Doomsday Prophecy in 1590.

St. Malachy was born in Armagh in 1094. His family name was O'Morgair. According to St. Bernard, he was of noble birth.

St. Malachy was baptized Maelmhaedhoc (Latinized as Malachy). He trained under Imhar O'Hagan, previously Abbot of Armagh. After a long course of studies, he was ordained priest by St. Cellach (Celsus) in 1119. He studied two more years, in Lismore, to perfect himself in sacred liturgy and theology. He then trained under St. Malchus. In 1123, he was chosen as Abbot of Bangor. A year later, he was consecrated Bishop of Connor. In 1132, he was promoted to the primacy of Armagh. Early in 1139, he journeyed to Rome via Scotland, England and France, visiting St. Bernard at Clairvaux. He petitioned Pope Innocent for palliums for the Sees of Armagh and Cashel and was appointed as legate for Ireland. On his return visit to Clairvaux, he obtained five monks for a foundation in Ireland, thus arose the great abbey of Mellifont in 1142. St. Malachy set out on a second journey to

Rome in 1148, but on arriving at Clairvaux, he fell sick and died in the arms of St. Bernard on November 2.

St. Bernard had praised St. Malachy's zeal for religion and said that he had restored the discipline of the Church which had grown lax during the intruded rule of a series of lay-abbots. St. Malachy was also said to have adopted the Roman liturgy.

Numerous miracles are attributed to St. Malachy and he was also said to have been endowed with the gift of prophecy. St. Malachy was canonized by Pope Clement III on July 6, 1199 and his feast is celebrated on November 3, in order not to clash with the Feast of All Souls.

The most famous prophecies about the popes are those attributed to St. Malachy. It was said that when he visited Rome in 1139, St. Malachy received the strange vision of the future wherein unfolded before his mind the long list of illustrious pontiffs who were to rule the Church until the end of time. It was said that St. Malachy gave a copy of his manuscript to Pope Innocent II to console him in the midst of his tribulations, and that the document remained unknown in the Roman Archives until its discovery in 1590. The manuscript was first published in 1595, by a Benedictine, Arnold de Wyon in his *Lignum Vitae*, a history of the Benedictine Order. Wyon claimed many are eager to read about the prophecies. There has been so much discussion about its authenticity given the silence of 400 years on the part of so many learned authors who had written about the popes. St. Bernard who wrote the "Life of St. Malachy," was also pretty quiet about it. Still, it was inconclusive to merely say that the prophecies about the pope were hidden in the Archives during those 400 years. St. Malachy died four centuries earlier before the prophecies appeared.

Wyon included both the alleged original prophecy which consisted of short, cryptic Latin phrases, as well as an interpretation applying the statements to historical popes.

Origin Theories

According to Abbe Cucherat, in 1871, St. Malachy was summoned to Rome in 1139 by Pope Innocent II to receive two wool palliums for the metropolitan sees of Armagh and Cashel. While in Rome, Malachy purportedly experienced a vision of future popes, which he recorded as a sequence of cryptic phrases. The manuscript was then allegedly deposited in the Vatican Secret Archives, and forgotten until its rediscovery in 1590, supposedly just in time for a papal conclave occurring at that time.

One theory to explain the prophecy's creation was put forward by the 17th-century French priest and encyclopaedist Louis Moreri among others. It was claimed that knowledge about the prophecies was spread around by supporters of Cardinal Girolamo Simoncelli in support of his bid to become pope during the 1590 conclave to replace Urban VII. In the prophecy, the pope following Urban VII is given the description "Ex antiquitate Ubis" (from the old city) and Simoncelli was from Orvieto, which in Latin is Urbeverantum, meaning old city. However, it was Niccolo Sfondrati who took the name Gregory XIV, who won. Proponents of the prophecies have attempted explanation by noting that Gregory XIV's father was a senator of the ancient city of Milan, and the word "senator" is derived from the Latin "senex" meaning old man, or that Milan is the "old city" in question, having been founded in c. 400 BCE.

The interpretation of the entries for pre-publication provided by Wyon involved linkage between the mottos and the popes' birthplaces, family names, coat-of-arms and pre-papal titles. For example, the first motto, Ex castro Tiberis (from a castle on the Tiber), fits Celestine II's birthplace in Citta di Castello, on the Tiber. Critics of the prophecy, such as M.J. O'Brien, a Catholic priest who authored an 1880 monograph on the prophecies, provided a more scathing assessment. O' Brien claimed that "These prophecies have served no purpose. They are absolutely meaningless. The Latin is bad. It is impossible to attribute such absurd triflings to any holy source. Their attempts at explaining the prophecies after 1590 are, I say with all respect, the sorriest trifling." Peter Bander, then Head of Religious Education at Wall Hall teacher training college wrote in 1969, "the most important factor, namely the popularity of the prophecies, particularly among the ordinary people (as distinct from scholars) makes them as relevant to the second half of the twentieth century as they have ever been."

CHAPTER 23

Popes 1590 to present

Post-appearance Popes (1590–present)				
Motto No.	Motto (*Translation*)	Regnal Name (Reign)	Name	Interpretations and Criticisms
Ex antiquitate Vrbis.		Gregorius. XIV.		
75.	Of the antiquity of the city / From the old city	**Gregory XIV** (1590–91)	Niccolò Sfondrati	This may have been intended to suggest that Cardinal Girolamo Simoncelli was destined to succeed Urban VII. Simoncello from Orvieto, which in Latin is *Urbs vetus* meaning old city. It was Niccolo Sfondrati, however, who took the name of Gregory XIV. Proponents of the prophecies noted that Gregory XIV's father was a senator of the ancient city of Milan,

				and the word *"senator"* is derived from the Latin *"senex,"* meaning old man, or that of Milan is the *"old city"* in question, having been founded c.400 BCE.
Pia ciuitas in bello.		Innocentius. IX.		
76.	Pious citizens in war	**Innocent IX** (1591)	Giovanni Antonio Facchinetti	Proponents included references to his birthplace of Bologna or title of Patriarch of Jerusalem
Crux Romulea.		Clemens. VIII.		
77.	Cross of Romulus	**Clement VIII** (1592–1605)	Ippolito Aldobrandini	Proponents included linking it to his embattled bend on his arms or the war between Catholic Ireland and Protestant England of his papacy.
Vndofus uir.				
78.	Wavy man	**Leo XI** (1605)	Alessandro Ottaviano De Medici	Proponents have suggested to relate this motto to this pope, relating it to his short reign "passing like a wave".
Gens peruerfa.				
79.	Wicked race	**Paul V** (1605–21)	Camillo Borghese	Proponents referred to the dragon and the eagle on Paul V's arms.
In tribulatione pacis.				
80.	In the trouble of peace	**Gregory XV** (1621–23)	Alessandro Ludovisi	"The prophet, up to 1590, did not deal in generalities."

Lilium et rofa.				
81.	Lily and rose	**Urban VIII** (1623–44)	Maffeo Barberini	In reference to the bees that do occur on his arms, to the fleur-de-lis of his native Florence, or to his dealings in France (the lily) and England (the rose).
Iucunditas crucis.				
82.	Delight of the cross	**Innocent X** (1644–55)	Giovanni Battista Pamphili	Raised to the pontificate around the time of the Feast of the Exaltation of the Cross.
Montium cuftos.				
83.	Guard of the mountains	**Alexander VII** (1655–67)	Fabio Chigi	His papal arms include six hills, though this was not an uncommon device, and this explanation would not account for the "guard" portion of the motto.
Sydus olorum.				
84.	Star of the swans	**Clement IX** (1667–69)	Giulio Rospigliosi	He had a room called the "chamber of swans" during the conclave.
De flumine magno.				
85.	From a great river	**Clement X** (1670–76)	Emilio Altieri	Tiber overflowed its banks at his birth, or as an obscure reference to his family name.
Bellua infatiabilis.				
86.	Insatiable beast	**Innocent XI** (1676–89)	Benedetto Odescalchi	Lion on Innocent XI's arms.
Pœnitentia gloriofa.				
87.	Glorious penitence	**Alexander VIII** (1689–91)	Pietro Ottoboni	Submission of the Gallican bishops. "There are glorious repentances during every pontificate."

Raſtrum in porta.				
88.	Rake in the door	**Innocent XII** (1691–1700)	Antonio Pignatelli	Some sources discussing the prophecy give Innocent XII's family name as "Pignatelli del Rastello", which would provide a clear way for proponents to connect this motto to this pope (*rastello* or *rastrello* is Italian for rake). Others, however, give the pope's family name as simply "Pignatelli", and indicate that it is difficult to find a satisfactory explanation to associate the pope with the motto.
Flores circundati.				
89.	Surrounded flowers	**Clement XI** (1700–21)	Giovanni Francesco Albani	A medal of Clement XI was created with the motto, "*Flores circumdati*", drawn from his description in the prophecies, which were widely circulated at that time.
De bona religione.				
90.	From good religion	**Innocent XIII** (1721–24)	Michelangelo dei Conti	In reference to the fact several popes had come from his family.
Miles in bello.				
91.	Soldier in War	**Benedict XIII** (1724–30)	Pietro Francesco Orsini	In reference to particular wars that occurred during Benedict XIII's pontificate, or a figurative war against decadence in favor of austerity.

Columna excelfa.				
92.	Lofty column	**Clement XII** (1730–40)	Lorenzo Corsini	Proponents of the prophecies have attempted to link this motto to Clement XII as an allusion to a statue erected in his memory or the use of two columns from the Pantheon of Agrippa in a chapel he built.
Animal rurale.				
93.	Country animal	**Benedict XIV** (1740–58)	Marcello Lambertini	Proponents have attempted to link this motto to this pope as a description of his "plodding ox" diligence.
Rofa Vmbriæ.				
94.	Rose of Umbria	**Clement XIII** (1758–69)	Carlo Rezzonico	As a reference to his elevation to sainthood of several Franciscans, to which order the motto can refer.
Vrfus uelox.				
95.	Swift bear (later misprinted as *Cursus velox* Swift Course or *Visus velox* Swift Glance)	**Clement XIV** (1769–74)	Lorenzo Giovanni Vincenzo Antonio Ganganelli	Proponents of the prophecies have struggled to provide a satisfactory explanation of this motto; some authors claim without evidence that the Ganganelli arms featured a running bear, but this is dubious.
Peregrin⁹ apoftolic⁹.[d]				
96.	Apostolic pilgrim	**Pius VI** (1775–99)	Giovanni Angelico Braschi	Proponents of the prophecies have suggested it is a reference to his long reign

Aquila rapax.				
97.	Rapacious eagle	**Pius VII** (1800–23)	Barnaba Chiaramonti	In reference to the eagle on the arms of Napoleon, whose reign as Emperor of the French took place during Pius' pontificate.
Canis & coluber.				
98.	Dog and adder	**Leo XII** (1823–29)	Annibale Sermattei della Genga	Proponents suggested that the dog and snake are allusions to his qualities of vigilance and prudence, respectively.
Vir religiofus.				
99.	Religious man	**Pius VIII** (1829–30)	Francesco Saverio Castiglioni	In reference to his papal name, or the fact that he was not the first pope from his family.
De balneis Ethruriæ.				
100.	From the baths of Etruria	**Gregory XVI** (1831–46)	Mauro, or Bartolomeo Alberto Cappellari	Proponents suggesting it is a reference to his membership in the Camaldolese Order, which was founded in the thirteenth century in a locality called *Balneum* (Bath) in Latin, in Etruria (Tuscany).
Crux de cruce.				
101.	Cross from cross	**Pius IX** (1846–78)	Giovanni Maria Mastai Ferretti	It has a reference to his difficulties ("crosses") with the House of Savoy, whose emblem is a cross. O'Brien notes, "A forger would be very disposed to chance some reference to a cross on account of its necessary connection

				with all popes as well as the probability of its figuring, in some form or other, on the pope's arms."
Lumen in cœlo.				
102.	Light in the sky	**Leo XIII** (1878–1903)	Gioacchino Pecci	Proponents of the prophecies have attempted to link this motto to Leo XIII by interpreting it as a reference to the star on his arms. O'Brien notes this coincidence would be much more remarkable had the prophecies referred to *sydus* (*star*), as they did when describing this same device on pre-publication Pope Innocent VII's arms.
Ignis ardens.				
103.	Burning fire	**Pius X** (1903–14)	Giuseppe Sarto	Interpreting it as a reference to his zeal.
Religio depopulata.				
104.	Religion destroyed	**Benedict XV** (1914–22)	Giacomo Della Chiesa	Proponents of the prophecies have attempted to link this motto to Benedict XV by interpreting it as a reference to World War I and the Russian Revolution, which occurred during his pontificate.
Fides intrepida.				
105.	Intrepid faith	**Pius XI** (1922–39)	Achille Ratti	Proponents of the prophecies have attempted to link this motto to Pius XI by interpreting it as a reference to his

				faith and actions during his pontificate: in 1937, the Pope strongly condemned Nazism and Communism (Encyclicals: Mit brennender Sorge, Divini Redemptoris). The end of his pontificate was dominated by speaking out against Hitler and Mussolini and defending the Catholic Church from intrusions into Catholic life and education.
Pastor angelicus.				
106.	Angelic shepherd	**Pius XII** (1939–58)	Eugenio Pacelli	Proponents of the prophecies have attempted to link this motto to Pius XII by interpreting it as a reference to his role during the holocaust.
Paſtor & nauta.				
107.	Shepherd and sailor	**John XXIII** (1958–63)	Angelo Giuseppe Roncalli	Proponents of the prophecies have attempted to link the "sailor" portion of this motto to John XXIII by interpreting it as a reference to his title Patriarch of Venice, a maritime city.
Flos florum.				
108.	Flower of flowers	**Paul VI** (1963–78)	Giovanni Battista Enrico Antonio Maria Montini	Proponents of the prophecies have attempted to link this motto to Paul VI by interpreting it as a reference to the fleurs-de-lis on his arms.

De medietate lunæ.				
109.	Of the half moon	**John Paul I** (1978)	Albino Luciani	Proponents of the prophecies have attempted to link this motto to John Paul I by referring to the light of the moon and interpreting his birth name as meaning "from the white light".
De labore solis.				
110.	From the labour of the sun / Of the eclipse of the sun[18][127]	**John Paul II** (1978–2005)	Karol Wojtyła	Proponents of the prophecies find significance in the occurrence of solar eclipses (elsewhere in the world) on the dates of John Paul II's birth (18 May 1920) and funeral (8 April 2005). Other attempts to link the pope to the motto have been "more forced", included drawing a connection to Copernicus (who formulated a comprehensive heliocentric model of the Solar System), as both were Polish and lived in Kraków for parts of their lives.
Gloria olivæ.				
111.	Glory of the olive.	**Benedict XVI** (2005–13)	Joseph Ratzinger	Benedict's choice of papal name is after Saint Benedict of Nursia, founder of the Benedictine Order, of which the Olivetans are one branch. Other explanations make reference to him as being a pope dedicated to peace and reconciliations of which the olive branch is the symbol.

In p[er]fecutione. extrema S.R.E. fedebit.		
	In the final persecution of the Holy Roman Church, there will sit.	In the *Lignum Vitae*, the line *"In persecutione extrema S.R.E. sedebit."* forms a separate sentence and paragraph of its own. It is viewed by some as a separate, incomplete sentence referring to additional popes between "glory of the olive" and "Peter the Roman" although on the other hand, the statement is seen as part of the "Peter the Roman" prophecy.
Petrus Romanus, qui pascet oues in multis tribulationibus: quibus tranfactis ciuitas fepticollis diruetur, & Iudex tremêdus iudicabit populum fuum. Finis.		
112.	Peter the Roman, who will pasture his sheep in many tribulations, and when these things are finished, the city of seven hills [i.e. Rome] will be destroyed, and the dreadful judge will judge his people. The End.	Many analyses of the prophecy note that it is open to the interpretation that additional popes would come between the "glory of the olive" and Peter the Roman. Popular speculation by proponents of the prophecy attach this prediction to Benedict XVI's successor. Proponents in internet forums have been striving, since Francis' election, to link him to the prophecy. Some theories include a vague connection with Francis of Assisi, whose father's name was Pietro (Peter).

Those who have undertaken to interpret and explain these symbolical prophecies have done so by discovering some trait, allusion, point or similitude in their application to the individual popes, either as to their country, their name, their coat of arms or insignia, their birth place, their talent or learning, the title of their cardinalate, the dignities which they held, etc. Examples were the prophecy concerning Urban VIII is Lilium et Rosa (the lily and the rose); Urban VIII was a native of Florence and on the arms of Florence was a fleur-de-lis; he had three bees emblazoned on his escutcheon and the bees gather honey from the lilies and roses. Pius VI, Peregrinus apostolicus (pilgrim pope) appears to be confirmed by his journey as pope into Germany, by his long career as pope and by his expatriation from Rome at the end of his pontificate. Those who have lived and followed the courses of events intelligently during the pontificates of Pius IX, Leo XIII and Pius X cannot fail to be impressed with the titles given to each of the prophecies of St. Malachy and their wonderful appropriateness: Crux de Cruce (Cross from a Cross) Pius IX, Lumen in Caelo (Light in the Sky) Leo XIII; Ignis ardens (Burning Fire) Pius X. It is said that there is something more than coincidence in the designations given to these popes so many a hundred years before their times.

CHAPTER 24

Petrus Romanus

What is most significant though is that in recent times, some interpreters of prophetic literature have drawn attention to the prophecy due to its imminent conclusion. If the list of descriptions and a list of historic popes since publications are matched on a one-to-one basis, Benedict XVI (2005-2013) would correspond to the second to the last of papal descriptions, the Gloria olivae (the glory of the olive). The longest and final verse predicts the Apocalypse: "*in persecione extrema S.R.E. sedebit, Petrus Romanus, qui pascet oves in multis tribulationibus quibus transactis civitas septicollis diruetur, & judex tremendous judicabit populum suum. Finis.*" This may be translated into English as:

> "*In the final persecution of the Holy Roman Church, there will sit (i.e. as bishop), Peter the Roman, who will pasture his sheep in many tribulations, and when these things are finished, the city of seven hills (i.e. Rome) will be destroyed and the dreadful judge will judge his people. The End.*"

Some interpret Pope Francis to be the last pope. "Romanus" can refer to his Italian heritage. Jose Mario Bergoglio emigrated from Italy to Argentina, in the 1920's, in search for a better life.

Several historians and interpreters entertain the possibility of unlisted popes between "glory of the olive" and "Peter the Roman" but specific characteristics fit Pope Francis to be "Petrus Romanus."

CHAPTER 25

St. Hildegard von Bingen

St. Hildegard was born at Bockelheim on the Nahe in 1098 and died on the Rupertsberg near Bingen on 1170. Her feast day was September 17. Not much is known of the family names of this great seeress and prophetess called the Sibyl of the Rhine. The early biographers give the first names of her parents as Hildebert and Mechtildis (or Mathilda), spoke of their nobility and riches, but gave no specifics of their lives. Later writers called the saint Hildegard of Bockelheim, of Rupertsberg, or of Bingen.

Legends would make her a Countess of Spanheim. J. May (Katholik xxxvii, 143) showed from letters and other documents that she probably belonged to the illustrious family of Stein, whose descendants are the Princes of Salm. Her father was a soldier in the service of Meginhard, Count of Spanheim. Hildegard was a weak and sickly child and thus received little education at home. Her parents were religiously inclined. They had promised the child to the service of God. At the age of eight, she was placed under the care of Jutta, sister of Count Meginhard, who lived as a recluse on the Benedictine cloister of Disenberg (or Disibodenberg, Mount of Disibod) in the Diocese of Speyer. Hildegard still received little instruction since she was much afflicted with sickness being frequently scarcely able to walk and often deprived even of the use of her eyes. She was however, taught to read and sing Latin psalms, enough for the chanting of the Divine office, but never learned to write. Eventually, she made her religious profession. Hildegard was invested with the habit of St. Benedictine when she was 15 years old. Jutta died in 1136 and Hildegard succeeded her. Numbers of aspirants flocked to the community and she decided to go to another locality, impelled also, as she says, of divine command. She chose Rupertsberg near Bingen on the left side of the Rhine, about 15 miles from Disenberg. Sometime around 1165, she found another convent on the south side of the Rhine, where one had already been established but was not successful. From her earliest years, she was favored with visions. She became reticent when she had found out that other people did not share her visions. "In my conversations, I would relate to future things, which I saw as if present, but noting the amazement of my listeners, I became more reticent." This went on to the end of her life. Jutta had noticed her gifts and made them known to a monk of a neighboring abbey. It seems though that nothing was done at that time. Having experience of visions even as a child, when she was about forty three years old then, she consulted her confessor, who in turn reported the matter to the archbishop of Mainz. A committee of theologians subsequently confirmed the authenticity of Hildegard's visions and a monk was assigned to help her record them in writing. Some of her nuns also frequently assisted her too. The finished work "Scivias" (1141-52), consists of 26 visions that are prophetic and apocalyptic in form and in their treatment of such topics as the church, the relationship between God and humanity, and redemption. About 1147 Hildegard left Disibodenberg to found a new convent at Rupertsberg, where she continued to exercise the gift of prophecy and to record her visions in writing. Crowds of people flocked to her from the neighborhood and from all parts of Germany and Gaul, to hear words of wisdom from her lips and to receive advice and help in corporal and spiritual ailments. These were not only from the common people but men and women of note in Church and State drawn by the report of her wisdom and sanctity. Thus, we read that Archbishop Heinrich of Mainz, Archbishop Eberhard of Salzburg and Abbot Ludwig of St. Eucharius at Trier paid her visits. St. Elizabeth of Schonau was a frequent visitor. Not did she give counsel at home but also abroad. In her last year, she had to undergo a very severe trial. In the cemetery adjoining her convent was a young man buried who had once been under excommunication. The ecclesiastical authorities of Mainz wanted the body removed. She did not consider herself bound to obey since the young man had received the last sacraments and was therefore supposed to have been reconciled to the Church. Sentence of interdict was placed on her convent by the chapter of Mainz, confirmed by the bishop, Christian (V) Buch then in Italy. After much worry and correspondence, she was successful in having the interdict removed. She died a holy death on September 17, 1179 and was buried in the Church at Rupertsberg.

Hildegard was greatly venerated in life and after death. Her biographer, Theodoric, calls her saint and that she had interceded for many miracles. The popes Gregory IX (1227-41) and Innocent IV (1243-54) ordered a process of information. This was repeated by Clement V (1305-14) and John XXII (1316-34). No formal canonization had taken place but her name was in the Roman martyrology and her feast was celebrated in the Dioceses of Speyer, Mainz, Trier and Limburg and also in the Abbey of Solesmes. When the convent on the Rupertsberg was destroyed in 1632, the relics of the saint were brought to Cologne and then to Eibingen. In 1857, an official recognition was made by the Bishop of Limburg and the relics were placed on an altar especially made for such purpose. On July 2, 1900 the cornerstone was laid for a new convent of St. Hildegard. The work was completed through the munificence of Prince Karl of Lowenstein. Benedictine nuns from St. Gabriel's at Prague entered the new home on September 17, 1904.

A talented poet and composer, Hildegard collected 77 of her lyric poems, each with a musical setting composed by her, in *Symphonia armonie celestium revelationum*. Her numerous other writings included lives of saints; two treatises on medicine and natural history, reflecting a quality of scientific observation rare at that period; and extensive correspondence, in which are found further prophecies and allegorical treatises. For her own amusement, she also contrived her own language. She traveled widely throughout Germany, evangelizing to large groups of people about her visions and religious insights. The first biography of St. Hildegard was written by contemporary monks Gottfried and Theodoric. St. Hildegard prophesied:

> *"The time is coming when princes and the people will renounce the authority of the Pope. Individual countries will prefer their own church rulers to the Pope. The German empire will be divided. Church property will be secularized. Priests will be persecuted. After the birth of the anti-Christ, heretics will preach their false doctrine undisturbed resulting in faith with doubts about their holy Catholic faith. Towards the end of the world, mankind will be purified through sufferings. This will be true especially of the clergy who will be robbed with all properties. When the clergy has adopted a simple manner of living, conditions will improve. A powerful wind will rise in the North carrying a heavy fog and the densest dust by divine command, and it will fill their throats and eyes so that they will cease their savaging and be stricken with great fear. After that, there will be so few men left that seven women will fight for one man, that they will say to the man, marry me to take the disgrace out upon me; for in those days, it will be*

a disgrace for a woman to be without a man as it is with the Jews by the Old Testament. Before the Comet comes, many nations, the good accepted, will be scorned with wanton famine. The great nation in the Ocean, that is inhabited by people of different tribes and descent by an earthquake, storm and tidal waves will be devastated. It will be divided and a great part, submerged. That nation will have many misfortunes at sea and lose its colonies in the East through a tiger and a lion. The Comet, by its tremendous pressure, will force much of the ocean and flood many countries, causing much want and many plagues. All coastal cities will be fearful and many of them will be destroyed by tidal waves and most of its living creatures will be killed. Even those who escape will die from a horrible disease. For none of these cities live according to the laws of God. Peace will return to Europe, when the white flower again, take possession of the throne of France. During this time of peace, people will be forbidden to carry weapons and irons will be used solely for agricultural implements and tools. Also, during this period, the soil will be very productive and many Jews and heathens and heretics will join the Church. The son of perdition who reign fiery few at times, will come at the end, during the duration of the world, at the times corresponding to the moment just before when the Sun disappears from the horizon. After having passed a licentious youth among many perverted men, and in a desert, she, being conducted by a demon disguised as an angel of light, the mother of the son of perdition will conceive and will give birth without knowing the *father. In another land, she will make men believe that her birth was some miracle saying that she had not appointed a spouse and she would ignore that. She will say how the infant she brought into the world had been formed in her womb. The people regard it as saint and will qualify to that title. The son of perdition is a very wicked beast, will put to death. those who do not believe in him; will associate with kings, priests, the great and the rich; who will mistake the humility and esteemed pride. He will finally subjugate the entire universe by his diabolic means. He will gain over many people and will tell them "***You are allowed to do all that you please****. Renounce the fasts. It suffices that you love me. I am your god." He will show them treasures and riches and he will permit them to riot in all sorts of festivities as they please. He will oblige them to practice circumcision and other Judaic observances and he will tell them, "Those who believe in me would receive pardon of their sins and will live with me eternally." He will reject baptism and evangelism, and he will reject, in derision, all the precepts the Holy Spirit has given to men of my part. Then he will say to his partisans, "Strike me with a sword and place my corpse in a proper shroud until the day of my resurrection." They will believe him to have really gone over to death and from his mortal wound, he will make a striking semblance of resurrection, after which he will impose himself a certain cipher, which he will say to be in place of salute. He will give it to all of his servators (sic) like the sign of our faith in heaven and he will command to adore it, concerning those who for the love of Jesus' name,* *will refuse to render this sacrilegious adoration to the son of perdition. He will put them to death amidst the cruelest formance (sic) but our Lord will defend his two witnesses, Enoch and Elias, whom he has reserved for those times. Their mission will be to combat the man of evil and reprimand him in the sight of the faithful whom he has seduced. They will have the virtue of operating the most brilliant miracles in all the places for the son of perdition has spread his evil doctrine. In the meanwhile, our Lord will permit this evildoer to put them to death but He will give them in heaven, the recompense of their travails. Later however, after the coming of Enoch and Elias, the anti-Christ will be destroyed and the Church will sing forth of unprecedented glory and the victims of the great era will be flung to return to the fold.*

On the note, where the son of perdition tells the world, "You are allowed to do as you please" almost stands synonymous to Pope Francis' call of "be messy."

A very direct criticism is as follows: *"Secondly, Pope Francis, love him or hate him, frequently likes to tell people to **make a mess,** "..meaning he wants to stir things up, and challenge people to do things they may not have considered." While it may be okay for college students making a mess at a local campus, the leader of the Catholic Church would be wise to note that "making a mess" at his level divides Christendom and emboldens enemies, especially when no clarifications are made on statements that stand at odds with Church teachings."*

Remember what it is said to be about prophecies. *"The veracity or accuracy of the fulfillment of these prophecies remains to be the litmus test to which all of them will be judged. They may sometimes be realized in part and in part may even run contrary to events. Due* to the conditional essence of some of them, they may or may not be fulfilled, or some fulfilled in one form or another."[92]

The man of sin, will be born of an ungodly woman, who from her infamy will have been initiated into occult sciences and the wiles of the demon. She will live in the desert of perverse men and abandon herself to crime with so much the greater ardor and she will think she is authorized thereby of the revelations of an angel and thus by the fire of burning concupiscence, she will conceive the son of perdition, without knowing by what father. And then she will be teaching that fornication is permitted, declaring herself holy and honored as a saint, but Lucifer, the old and cunning serpent, will find the fruit of her womb with his infernal spirit and entirely possess the fruit of sin. Now when he shows them the age of manhood, he will set himself up as a new master, and teach perverse doctrine. Soon he will revolt against the saints, and he will reprise such great power, that in the madness of his pride, he would raise himself above the clouds as in the beginning. Satan said, I will be like unto the Most High, and fell. So, in those days, he will fall in the person of his son "I am the savior of the world." He will ally himself with the kings, the princes and all the powerful ones of the Earth. He will condemn humility and will extol all the doctrines of pride. His magic act will feign the most astonishing prodigies. He will disturb the atmosphere; command thunder and tempest, produce hail and horrible lightnings. He'll move mountains and dry up streams; reanimate the weathered adventures of the forests. His art will be practiced upon the elements but chiefly upon men.; will exhaust his infernal power. He will seem to take away health and restore it. How so? By sending some possessed souls into a dead body; to move it for a time but these resurrections will be of short duration. At the sight of these things, many will be terrified and will believe in him and some preserving their primitive faith will nevertheless count

---

[92] "Prophecy." Catholic.com. Retrieved from https://www.catholic.com/encyclopedia/prophecy. May 17, 2021.

the favor of the man of sin or fear his displeasure. So many will be led astray among those shutting the interior eyes of their soul will habitually in exterior things. After the anti-Christ has ascended the high mountain and been destroyed by Christ, many erring souls will return to the truth and men will make rapid progress in the ways of holiness. Nothing good will enter into him, nor be able to be in him, for he will be nourished in diverse and secret places; lest he should be known by man, and he will be imbued by diabolical arts and he will be hidden until he is full of rage, nor will he show the perversities which will be in him till he knows himself to be full and super abundant in all his inequities. He will appear to produce rainbows, lightnings, thunder and hail, to tumble mountains and dry up streams, to strip the verdor of trees, of forests and restore sick or will; to chase out demons and at times even to resurrect the dead, making a cadaver to move like it was alive but this kind of resurrection will never endure beyond a little time for the glory of God will not suffer it. Ostensibly, he will be murdered, spill his blood and die. With bewilderment and consternation, mankind will learn that he is not dead but is awakened from his death sleep. From the beginning of his course, many battles and many things contrary to the law of dispensation will arise and charity will be extinguished in men. In them will also arise bitterness and harshness and there will be so many heresies, that heretics will preach their errors openly and certainly. There will be so much doubt and incertitude in the Catholic faith of Christians that men shall be in doubt of what God be invoked and many signs will appear in the Sun and the moon and in the stars and waters and in other elements and creatures. So that, as if we were in a picture, future events will be foretold in their potency. Then, so much sadness shall occupy men at that time, they shall be led to die as if for nothing but those who are perfect in the Catholic faith will await in the great contrition where God wills to ordain. In there, great tribulations shall proceed in this way while the Son of perdition will open his mouth, and the words of falsehood and his deceptions, heaven and earth shall trample together, but after the fall of the anti-Christ, the glory of the Son of God shall be increased. As soon as he is born, he will have teeth and pronounce blasphemies. In short, he will be a born devil. He will emit fearful cries, work miracles and wallow in luxury and advice. He will have brothers who are also devils incarnate. At the age of 12, they will distinguish themselves in brilliant achievements. They will command an armed force, which will be supported by the infernal legions. After the son of perdition has accomplished all of his evil designs, he will call together, all of his believers and tell them that he wishes to ascend to heaven. At the moment of his ascension, a thunderbolt will strike him into the ground and he will die. The mountain where he was established for the operation of his ascension, in an instant, will be covered by a thick cloud which emits an unbearable odor of truly infernal corruption. At the sight of his body, the eyes of a great number of persons will open and they will be made to see their immiserable (sic) error. After the sorrowful defeat of the son of perdition, the spouse of my Son, who is the Church, will shine with the glory without equal and the victims of error will be impressed to reenter the sheepfold. As to the day, after the fall of the anti-Christ, when the world will end, Man must not seek to know for he can never learn it; that secret the Father has reserved for Himself.[93]

Similarity with the La Salette Prophecy

The prophecies of La Salette sounds very much like the prophecies of St. Hildegard of Bingen in reference to the anti-Christ.

"It will be at this time that the Antichrist will be born of a Hebrew nun, a false virgin who will be in communication with the ancient serpent, master of impurity; his father will be a bishop."

---

[93] "We were warned Prophecies of St. Hildegard of Bingen." YouTube. Retrieved from https://www.youtube.com/watch?v=MBIRupa9CHc. May 18, 2021.

"At birth he will vomit blasphemies, he will have teeth; in a word, this will be the devil incarnate; he will utter terrifying cries, he will work wonders, he will live only on impurities. He will have brothers who, although not incarnate devils like himself, will be children of evil; at the age of twelve, they will be noted for the valiant victories they will win; soon they will each be at the head of armies, assisted by legions from hell.

"The seasons will be changed, the earth will produce only bad fruits, the heavenly bodies will lose the regularity of their movements, the moon will reflect only a feeble reddish light; water and fire will lend convulsive motions to the earth's sphere, causing mountains, cities, etc., to be swallowed up.

"Rome will lose the Faith and become the seat of the Antichrist.

"The demons of the air, together with the Antichrist, will work great wonders on the earth and in the air, and men will become ever more perverted. God will take care of His faithful servants and mend of good will; the Gospel will be preached everywhere all peoples and all nations will have knowledge of the Truth.

Similarity with the Fatima Third Message

The prophecies of St. Hildegard of Bingen also sounds like the Fatima Third message.

And we saw in an immense light that is God: 'something similar to how people appear in a mirror when they pass in front of it' a Bishop dressed in White 'we had the impression that it was the Holy Father'. Other Bishops, Priests, men and women Religious going up a steep mountain, at the top of which there was a big Cross of rough-hewn trunks as of a cork-tree with the bark; before reaching there the Holy Father passed through a big city half in ruins and half trembling with halting step, afflicted with pain and sorrow, he prayed for the souls of the corpses he met on his way; having reached the top of the mountain, on his knees at the foot of the big Cross

172

he was killed by a group of soldiers who fired bullets and arrows at him, and in the same way there died one after another the other Bishops, Priests, men and women Religious, and various lay people of different ranks and positions.

CHAPTER 26

Anne Catherine of Emmerich

Anne Katharina Emmerich (8 September 1774-9 February 1824) was a Roman Catholic Augustinian Canoness Regular of Windesheim, mystic, Marian visionary, ecstatic and stigmatist. She was born in Flamschen, a farming community at Coesfeld in the Diocese of Munster, Westphalia, Germany, where she had been a nun and later became bedridden and died at age 49 in Dulmen. Emmerich is noted for her visions on the life and passion of Jesus Christ, revealed to her by the Blessed Virgin Mary under religious ecstasy. She was beatified on October 3, 2004 by St. John Paul.

Emmerich was born into a family of poor farmers. She had nine brothers and sisters. The family's surname was derived from an ancestral town. She helped with house and farm work at an early age. Her schooling was rather brief. All those who knew her noticed that she felt drawn to prayer at an early age. A twelve, she started to work at a large farm in the area for three years. She later learned to be a seamstress and worked as such for several years.

She applied for admission to various convents, but she was rejected. She could not afford to pay a dowry. Eventually, the Poor Clares in Münster agreed to accept her, on the condition that she would learn to play the organ. She went to the organist

Söntgen in Coesfeld to study music and learn to play the organ. The poverty of the Söntgen family prompted her to work there and to sacrifice her small savings in an effort to help them. Later, one of the Sontgen daughters entered the convent with her.

In 1802, at the age of 28, Emmerich and her friend Klara Sontgen finally managed to join the Augustinian nuns at the convent of Agnetenberg in Dulmen. Emmerich took her vows the following year. In the convent, she became known for her strict observance of the order's rule; but from the start to 1811, she was often quite ill and had to endure great pain. At times her zeal and strict adherence to rules bothered some of the more tepid sisters. They were puzzled by her weak health and religious ecstasies.

When Jerome Bonaparte, King of Westphalia, suppressed the convent in 1812, she found refuge in a widow's house.

Blessed Anne's Stigmata and Visions

In early 1813, marks of the stigmata were reported on Emmerich's body. She also had a cross on her breastbone with the unusual shape of a "Y" similar to a cross in the local church of Coesfeld, which was understood as an exterior manifestation of being a stigmatist. The parish priest called in two doctors to examine her. When word of the phenomenon spread three months later, the priest notified the vicar general. With the news causing considerable talk in the town, the ecclesiastical authorities conducted a lengthy investigation. Many doctors wished to examine the case. Although efforts were made to discourage the curious, there were visitors whose rank or status gained them entry. During this time, the poet and romanticist Clemens Brentano first visited. He later wrote two books about her visions but was criticized about its authenticity and dismissed as "well-intentioned fraud."

At the end of 1818, the periodic bleeding of Emmerich's hands and feet had stopped and the wounds had closed. While many in the community viewed the stigmata as real, others considered Emmerich an imposter. They accused her of conspiring with her associates to perpetuate a fraud. In August 1819, the civil authorities intervened and moved Emmerich to a different house. She was kept under observation for three weeks. The members of the commission could find no evidence of fraud and were divided in their opinions.

Emmerich was beatified on October 3, 2004 by Pope John Paul II. The Vatican however, focused on her own personal piety rather than the writings of Clemens Brentano.

The following are what she wrote down:

March 22, 1820

I saw very clearly the errors, the aberrations and the countless sins of men. I saw the folly and the wickedness of their actions, against all truth and all reason. Priests were among them, and I gladly endured my suffering so that they may return to a better mind.[94]

April 12, 1820

"I had another vision of the great tribulation. It seems to me that a concession was demanded from the clergy which could not be granted. I saw many older priests, especially one, who wept bitterly. A few younger ones were also weeping. But others, and the lukewarm among them readily did what was demanded. It was as if people were splitting into two camps..."[95]

---

[94] "Blessed Anne Catherine Emmerich's Prophecy on Two Popes" These Last Days News, June 9, 2016. Retrieved from https://www.tldm.org/news29/blessed-anne-catherine-emmerichs-prophecy-on-two-popes.htm. May 18, 2021.

[95] Ibid.

May 13, 1820

MARY OF THE ROTUNDA AND THE CHAPEL OF THE PROTESTANT EMBASSY, AT ROME May 13, 1820

Last night, from eleven to three, I had a most wonderful vision of two churches and two Popes and a variety of things, ancient and modern. I shall relate, as well as I can, all that I remember of it. My angel guardian came and told me that I must go to Rome and take two things to the Pope, but I cannot now recall what they were— perhaps it is the Will of God that I should forget them. I asked my angel how I could make so long a journey, sick as I was. But when I was told that I should make it without difficulty, I no longer objected. An odd-looking vehicle appeared before me, flat and slight, with only two wheels, the flooring red with white edges. I saw no horses. I was gently lifted and laid on it and, at the same instant, a snow-white, luminous child flew toward me and seated himself at my feet. He reminded me of the Patience child in green, so sweet, so lovely, and perfectly transparent. He was to be my companion; he was to console and take care of me. The wagon was so light and smooth that at first, I was afraid of slipping off; but it began to move very gently of itself without horses, and I saw a shining human figure going on ahead.[96]

The journey did not seem long, although we crossed countries, mountains, and great waters. I knew Rome the instant we reached it, and I was soon in the presence of the Pope. I know not now whether he was sleeping or praying, but I had to say two things to him, or give him two things, and I shall have to go to him once again to announce a third. Then I had a wonderful vision. Rome suddenly appeared as in the early ages, and I saw a Pope (Boniface IV) and

---

[96] "Blessed Anne Catherine Emmerich's Prophecy on Two Popes" These Last Days News, June 9, 2016. Retrieved from https://www.tldm.org/news29/blessed-anne-catherine-emmerichs-prophecy-on-two-popes.htm. May 18, 2021.

an emperor whose name I knew not (Phocas). I could not find my way in the city, all was so different, even the sacred ceremonies; but yet I recognized them as Catholic. I saw a great round building like a cupola— it was a pagan temple full of beautiful idols. It had no windows, but in the dome was an opening with a contrivance for keeping out the rain. It seemed as if all the idols that ever existed were gathered together there in every conceivable posture. Many of them were very beautiful, and others exceedingly odd; there were even some of geese which received divine honor. In the center of the building stood a very high pyramid formed entirely of those images. I saw no idolatrous worship at the time of which I speak, although the idols were still carefully preserved. I saw messengers from Pope Boniface going to the emperor and petitioning for the temple to be changed into a Christian church. I heard the latter declaring distinctly that the Pope should allow the ancient statues to remain, though he might erect therein the Cross to which the highest honors should be paid. This proposal, as it seemed to me, was made not wickedly, but in good faith. I saw the messengers return with the answer and Boniface reflecting as to how he might in some measure conform to the emperor's will. While he was thus deliberating, I saw a good, pious priest in prayer before the crucifix. He wore a long white robe with a train, and an angel hovered by his side. Suddenly he arose, went straight to Boniface, and told him that he should by no means accede to the emperor's proposal. Messengers were then dispatched to the emperor, who now consented to the temple's being entirely cleared. Then I saw his people come and take numbers of the statues to the imperial city; but still many remained in Rome. Then I saw the consecration of the temple, at which ceremony the holy martyrs assisted with Mary at their head. The altar was not in the center of the building, but against the wall. I saw more than thirty wagon-loads of sacred relics brought into the church.[97]

---

[97] Ibid.

I saw also the relationship between the two popes…I saw how baleful would be the consequences of this false church. I saw it increase in size; heretics of every kind came into the city (of Rome). The local clergy grew lukewarm and I saw a great darkness… Then the vision seemed to extend on every side. Whole Catholic communities were being oppressed, harassed, confined and deprived of their freedom. I saw many churches close down, great miseries everywhere, wars and bloodshed. A wild and ignorant mob took to violent action. But it did not last long."[98]

"*I had another vision of the great tribulation. It seems to me that a concession was demanded from the clergy which could not be granted. I saw many older priests, especially one who wept bitterly. A few younger ones were also weeping. But others, and the lukewarm among them, readily did what was demanded. It was as if people were splitting into two camps.*[99]

I see the Holy Father in great anguish. He lives in a palace other than before and he admits only a limited number of friends near him. I fear that the Holy Father will suffer many more trials before he dies.

"*Once more, I saw that the Church of Peter was undermined by a plan evolved by the secret sect (Freemasons), while storms were damaging it. But I saw also that help was coming when distress had reached its peak. I saw again the Blessed Virgin ascend on the Church and spread her mantle (over it).*"[100]

I see that the false Church of darkness is making progress and I see the dreadful influence it has on the people. The Holy Father and the Church are verily in so great a distress that one must implore God night and day…"

---

[98] "Blessed Anne Catherine Emmerich's Prophecy on Two Popes" These Last Days News, June 9, 2016. Retrieved from https://www.tldm.org/news29/blessed-anne-catherine-emmerichs-prophecy-on-two-popes.htm. May 18, 2021.

[99] Ibid.

[100] Ibid.

"Many of them were enclosed in the walls and others could be seen through round openings covered with something like glass.

When I had witnessed this vision even in the smallest details, I saw again the present Pope and the dark church of his time in Rome. It seemed to be a large, old house like a town hall with columns in front. I saw no altar in it, but only benches, and in the middle of it something like a pulpit."

"They had preaching and singing, but nothing else, and only very few attended it. And lo, a most singular sight! Each member of the congregation drew an idol from his breast, set it up before him, and prayed to it. It was as if each man drew forth his secret thoughts or passions under the appearance of a dark cloud which, once outside, took some definite form." [101]

"They were precisely such figures as I had seen around the neck of the illicit bride in the Nuptial House, figures of men and animals. The god of one was short and broad with a crisp head and numerous, outstretched arms ready to seize and devour all in its reach; that of another was quite small with miserable, shrunken limbs; another had merely a block of wood upon which he gazed with rolling eyes; this one had a horrible animal; that one, a long pole. The most singular part of it was that the idols filled the place; the church, although the worshippers were so few, was crowded with idols. When the service was over, everyone's god re-entered into his breast. The whole church was draped in black, and all that took place in it was shrouded in gloom." [102]

In light of this wooden idol, it seems it has astounding reference to Pachamama, "Mother Earth" celebrated at the Vatican prior to the Amazon Synod.

Pope Francis definitely got some very sharp criticism.

---

[101] Ibid.

[102] "Blessed Anne Catherine Emmerich's Prophecy on Two Popes" These Last Days News, June 9, 2016. Retrieved from https://www.tldm.org/news29/blessed-anne-catherine-emmerichs-prophecy-on-two-popes.htm. May 18, 2021.

"But these are disturbing days. In particular, I refer to the blessing and welcoming of a pagan idol – a demon – by Pope Francis into the Vatican, and St. Peter's Basilica itself in October, 2019 as part of the Amazon Synod. Many better and holier men than me have written about this scandalous event. I refer chiefly to Archbishop Vigano, whose August 2018 Testimony exposed to an unprecedented degree the amount of corruption and perversion currently at work in the Church, and at the behest of many of Her most powerful prelates, including Pope Francis himself. The abomination of idolatrous rites has entered the sanctuary of God," he said in a November 2019 interview on the Pachamama scandal. In March of 2020, he called on Pope Francis to "convert" repent for this sacrilegious act. Likewise, Catholic theologian Douglas Farrow has written two compelling pieces on the Amazon Synod, *The Amazon Synod Is a Sign of the Times* and *Reading the Signs of the Times.* Cardinal Raymond Burke has said that "diabolical forces entered St. Peter's Basilica through the idolatrous Pachamama event. Finally, 100+ Catholic theologians, priests and laymen signed a Protest Against Pope Francis's Sacrilegious Acts in response to the Pachamama fiasco."[103]

Then I saw the connection between the two Popes and the two temples. I am sorry that I have forgotten the numbers, but I was shown how weak the one had been in adherents and human support, but how strong in courage to overturn so many gods (I knew the number) and to unite so many different forms of worship into one; and, on the contrary, how strong in numbers and yet how irresolute in action was the other since, in authorizing the erection of false temples, he had allowed the only true God, the

[103] "Pachamama Is A Demon: Testimony from A Missionary" Joshua Charles. Retrieved from https://www.joshuatcharles.com/blog/2020/4/24/pachamama-is-a-demon-testimony-from-missionaries. May 19, 2021.

only true religion to be lost among so many false gods and false religions.[104]

It was also shown me that those pagans humbly adored gods other than themselves, and that they would have been willing to admit in all simplicity the only God, the Most Holy Trinity. Their worship was preferable to that of those who adore themselves in a thousand idols to the total exclusion of Our Lord. The picture was favorable to the early ages, for in them idolatry was on the decrease, while in our days it is just the contrary. I saw the fatal consequences of this counterfeit church; I saw it increase; I saw heretics of all kinds flocking to the city. I saw the ever-increasing tepidity of the clergy, the circle of darkness ever widening."[105]

"And now the vision became more extended. I saw in all places Catholics oppressed, annoyed, restricted, and deprived of liberty, churches were closed, and great misery prevailed everywhere with war and bloodshed."

Churches being closed indeed happened. Not only in Rome but around the world. In Rome, in an unprecedented manner in modern times, Roman Catholic churches were ordered closed because of the coronavirus pandemic. The decree given by Cardinal Angelo De Donatis, Pope Francis' vicar for the Rome archdiocese, will remain in effect until at least April 3, 2020. There are more than 900 parochial and historic churches in Rome.[106]

---

[104] "Blessed Anne Catherine Emmerich's Prophecy on Two Popes" These Last Days News, June 9, 2016. Retrieved from https://www.tldm.org/news29/blessed-anne-catherine-emmerichs-prophecy-on-two-popes.htm. May 18, 2021.

[105] Ibid.

[106] "Rome Catholic Churches ordered closed due to coronavirus, unprecedented in modern times"
Reuters. Retrieved from https://www.reuters.com/article/us-health-coronavirus-italy-rome-churche/rome-catholic-churches-ordered-closed-due-to-coronavirus-unprecedented-in-modern-times-idUSKBN20Z3BU. May 19, 2021.

"I saw rude, ignorant people offering violent resistance, but this state of things lasted not long. Again, I saw in vision St. Peter's undermined according to a plan devised by the secret sect while, at the same time, it was damaged by storms; but it was delivered at the moment of greatest distress. Again, I saw the Blessed Virgin extending her mantle over it.[107]

"In this last scene, I saw no longer the reigning Pope, but one of his successors, a mild, but very resolute man who knew how to attach his priests to himself and who drove far from him the bad. I saw all things renewed and a church which reached from earth to Heaven. I saw one of the twelve new apostles in the person of the young priest whom the unchaste bride wanted to marry."[108]

"It was a very comprehensive vision and portrayed anew all that had been previously shown me regarding the Church's destiny. On another occasion, I had a vision of the Vicar-General's stanch resistance to secular power in behalf of the interests of the Church. The affair covered him with glory, though upon some other points he was to blame. I was told that I should have to go again to the Pope; but when all this will take place I cannot say." [109]

May 13, 2020 is the 200th anniversary of one of the most historically and mystically significant prophetic visions any Saint has had in the history of the Church. Aside from its accuracy, the prophecy also speaks to us on in our own time of chaos in Church and State. A time in which there are two popes at the same time. There also has not been any anti-pope in the last 570 years, the

---

[107] "Blessed Anne Catherine Emmerich's Prophecy on Two Popes" These Last Days News, June 9, 2016. Retrieved from https://www.tldm.org/news29/blessed-anne-catherine-emmerichs-prophecy-on-two-popes.htm. May 18, 2021.

[108] Ibid.

[109] "Blessed Anne Catherine Emmerich's Prophecy on Two Popes" These Last Days News, June 9, 2016. Retrieved from https://www.tldm.org/news29/blessed-anne-catherine-emmerichs-prophecy-on-two-popes.htm. May 18, 2021.

last being Felix V (Duke Amadeus VIII of Savory) who falsified the papacy, from Nov. 5, 1439 to April 7, 1449 A. D.

The fact that Blessed Anne Catherine Emmerich had this vision, in particular, regarding a wicked pope in Rome establishing worship for all gods in the Church, it has been 200 years to the day that Pope Francis has called upon all religions to pray together. The date of May 13, 2020 is not coincidental, unless of course it was willed by Pope Francis precisely to indicate that he recognizes himself as the Anti-Christ in this vision.

July 1820

"I saw the Holy Father surrounded by traitors and in great distress about the Church. He had visions and apparitions in his hour of greatest need. I saw many good pious Bishops; but they were weak and wavering, their cowardice often got the upper hand... Then I saw darkness spreading around and people no longer seeking the true Church."

When Pope Francis signed the Abu Dhabi document on February 4, 2019 it could be said that they are no longer seeking the true Church. On one hand, it could be said they have a lofty ideal. Both the Pope and the Grand Imam have stated their mission statement for a more unified world, free from the scourge of terrorism, with equal rights for women and appreciation for all religious and places of worship, should be the "object of research and reflection in all schools, universities and institutes of formation" to helping to educate new generations to bring goodness and peace to others.[110]

The Pope and the Grand Imam of Al Azhar have initiated the Human Fraternity Document making a clarion call on people

---

[110] "What is the Human Fraternity Document Signed in Abu Dhabi" The National. Retrieved from https://www.thenationalnews.com/uae/the-pope-in-the-uae/what-is-the-human-fraternity-document-signed-in-abu-dhabi-1.821882. May 20, 2021.

across the globe to unite to bring about inter-faith harmony and spread a vital message of peace. The Document would be the blueprint to "guide future generations" to advance "a culture of mutual respect" spanning all nationalities, backgrounds and beliefs.[111] It was unveiled after Pope Francis and Dr Ahmed Al Tayeb, revered figures in the Catholic and Muslim faiths, met at the Global Conference of Human Fraternity in Abu Dhabi. The Document was signed at the Founder Memorial in the capital in the presence of Sheik Mohammed bin Rashid and Sheik Mohamed bin Zayed in the AL Azhar Muslim University, in Cairo, Egypt on February 4, 2019.

In another perspective, Pope Francis has manifested heresy. Some believed that the Document on Human Fraternity contains statements that are "directly contrary to the Catholic faith." This has serious theological and canonical implications. Given its gravity, focus is proposed on the statement "The pluralism and the diversity of religions… are willed by God and His wisdom." This formally contradicts a Catholic doctrine.

God cannot desire the existence of false religions because He cannot want both truth and error, good and evil. If that were so, He would be a contradictory being and a contradictory being cannot be God, Who is eternal Wisdom, supreme truth and goodness.

It would be incoherent if God willed a Trinitarian religion like the Catholic and at the same time, an anti-Trinitarian religion one like Islam, modern Judaism, or, for that matter, religions like Buddhism and Animism that do not believe in a personal God. To give just two examples of incompatibility between the one true religion and the many false ones: God cannot approve monogamy and polygamy, divorce and the indissolubility of marriage simultaneously.

---

[111] "What is the Human Fraternity Document Signed in Abu Dhabi" The National. Retrieved from https://www.thenationalnews.com/uae/the-pope-in-the-uae/what-is-the-human-fraternity-document-signed-in-abu-dhabi-1.821882. May 20, 2021.

Both human reason and divine Revelation reject contradiction in God:" Thou shalt not have strange gods before me." (Exodus 20:3). The reason that God allows the existence of false religions and other evils is not because He wishes. Pope Leo XIII explained clearly in his encyclical Libertas Praestantissima:

"God Himself in His providence, though infinitely good and powerful, permits evil to exist in the world, partly that greater good may not be impeded, and partly that greater evil may not ensue."[112]

Dr. John Lamont believes that Pope Francis has taken on a public repudiation of the Catholic faith given the normal meaning of the statement about pluralism and diversity of religion as willed by God in His wisdom. He believes this statement is directly contrary to the Catholic faith.

August to October, 1820

"I see more martyrs, not now but in the future...I saw the secret sect relentlessly undermining the great Church. Near them, I saw a horrible beast coming up from the sea...All over the world, good and devout people especially the clergy were harassed, oppressed and put into prison. I had the feeling that they would become martyrs one day."

"When the Church had been for the most part destroyed (by the secret sect Freemasons) and when only the sanctuary and altar were still standing, I saw the wreckers enter the Church with the Beast. There was a Woman of noble carriage who seemed to be with child because she walked slowly. At this sight, the enemies were terrorized and the Beast could not take another step forward. It projected its neck towards the Woman as if to devour her, but the Woman turned

---

[112] "Theological and Canonical Implications of the Declaration Signed by Pope Francis in Abu Dhabi." The American Society for the Defense of Tradition, Family and Property. Retrieved from https://www.tfp.org/theological-and-canonical-implications-of-the-declaration-signed-by-pope-francis-in-abu-dhabi/ May 20, 2021.

about and bowed down (towards the altar), her head touching the ground. Thereupon, I saw the Beast taking to flight towards the sea again, and the enemies were fleeing in the greatest confusion.... Then, I saw in the great distance great legion approaching. In the foreground, I saw a man on a white horse. Prisoners were set free and joined them. All enemies were pursued. Then, I saw that the Church was being promptly rebuilt and she was more magnificent than ever before..."

August 10, 1820

"I see the Holy Father in great anguish. **He lives in a palace other than before** and he admits only a limited number of friends near him. I fear that the Holy Father will suffer many more trials before he dies. I see that the false Church of darkness is making progress and I see the dreadful influence it has on the people. The Holy Father and the Church are verily in so great a distress that one must implore God night and day..."

Pope Francis is said to reside in Domus Sanctae Marthae. In Italian, it is Casa Santa Marta. It is a building adjacent to St. Peter's Basilica in Vatican City. It was completed in 1996, during the pontificate of Pope John Paul II and was named after Martha of Bethany, who was sibling to Mary and Lazarus of Bethany. The building functions as a guest house for clergy having business with the Holy See and as the temporary residence of members of the College of Cardinals while involved in a papal conclave to elect a new pope. Pope Francis has declined to use the papal apartments in the Apostolic Palace and has lived in a suite in the building since his election in March 2013.

I have been told to pray much for the Church and the Pope... The people must pray earnestly for the extirpation (rooting out) of the dark church."

"Last night I was taken to Rome where the Holy Father immersed in his sorrow is still hiding to elude dangerous demands *(made upon him). He is still very weak and exhausted by sorrows, cares and prayers. He can now trust but few people. That is mainly why he is hiding. But he still has with him an aged priest who has much simplicity and godliness. He is his friend and because of his simplicity, they did not think it would be worth removing him. But this man receives many graces from God. He sees and notices a great many things which he faithfully reports to the Holy Father. It was required of me to inform him while he was praying, of the traitors and evil doers who were to be found among the high-ranking servants living close to him, so that he might be made aware of it.*

Could this aged priest be Pope Benedict XVI?

August 25, 1820

I do not know in what manner I was taken to Rome last night, but I found myself near the Church of St Mary Major, and I saw many poor people who were greatly distressed and worried because the Pope was to be seen nowhere, and also on account of the restlessness and the alarming rumors in the city. These people did not seem to expect the Church doors to open; they only wanted to pray outside. An inner urging had left them there individually. But I was in the Church, and I opened the doors. They came in, surprised and frightened because the doors had opened. It seems to me that I was behind the door, and they could not see me. There was no office on in the Church. But the sanctuary lamps were lit. The people prayed quite peacefully..."

"Then I saw an apparition of the Mother of God, and she said that the tribulation would be very great. She added that people must pray fervently with outstretched arms, be it only long enough to say three Our Fathers. This was the way her Son prayed for them on the Cross. They must rise at twelve at night, and pray in this manner; and they must keep coming to the Church. They must pray above all for the Church of Darkness to leave Rome..."

"She (the Holy Mother) said a great many others things that it pains

me to relate: she said that if only one priest could offer the bloodless sacrifice as worthily and with the same disposition as the Apostles, he could avert all the disasters (that are to come). To my knowledge the people in the Church did not see the apparition, but they must have been stirred by something supernatural, because as soon as the Holy Virgin had said that they must pray God with outstretched arms, they all raised their arms. These were all good and devout people, and they did not know where help and guidance should be sought. There were no traitors and enemies among them, yet they were afraid of one another. One can judge thereby what the situation was like."

September 10, 1820

"I saw the Church of St Peter: it has been destroyed but for the Sanctuary and the main altar. St Michael came down into the Church, clad in his suit of armor, and he paused, threatening with his sword and number of unworthy pastors who wanted to enter. That part of the Church which had been destroyed was promptly fenced in with light timber so that the Divine office might be celebrated as it should. Then, from all over the world came priests and laymen and they rebuilt the stone walls, since the wreckers had been unable to move the heavy foundation stones. And then I saw that the Church was being promptly rebuilt and She was more magnificent than ever before..."

September 12, 1820

"I saw a strange church being built against every rule...No angels were supervising the building operations. In that church, nothing came from high above...There was only division and chaos. It is probably a church of human creation, following the latest fashion, as well as the new heterodox Church of Rome [one world church of the False Prophet], which seems of the same kind..."

I saw again the strange big church that was being built there (in Rome). There was nothing holy in it. I saw this just as I saw a movement led by Ecclesiastics to which contributed angels, saints and other Christians. But there (in the strange big church) all the work was being done mechanically (i.e., according to set rules and formula). Everything was being done, according to human reason. I saw all sorts of people, things, doctrines, and opinions. There was something proud, presumptuous, and violent about it, and they seemed to be very successful. I did not see a single Angel nor a single saint helping in the work. But far away in the background, I saw the seat of a cruel people armed with spears, and I saw a laughing figure which said: 'Do build it as solid as you can; we will put it to the ground.

I saw that many of the instruments in the new Church, such as spears and darts, were meant to be used against the living Church. Everyone dragged in something different: clubs, rods, pumps, cudgels, puppets, mirrors, trumpets, horns bellows – all sorts of things. In the cave below (the sacristy) some people kneaded bread, but nothing came of it; it would not rise. The men in the little mantles brought wood to the steps of the pulpit to make a fire. They puffed and blew and labored hard, but the fire would not burn. All they produced was smoke and fumes. Then they broke a hole in the roof and ran up a pipe, but the smoke would not rise, and the whole place became black and suffocating. Some blew the horns so violently that the tears streamed from their eyes. All in this church belonged to the earth, returned to the earth. All was dead, the work of human skill, a church of the latest style, a church of man's invention like the new heterodox church in Rome."

September 27, 1820

"I saw deplorable things: they were gambling, drinking, and talking in church; they were also courting women. All sorts of abominations were perpetrated there. Priests allowed everything and said Mass with much irreverence. I saw that few of them were

still godly, and only a few had sound views on things. I also saw Jews standing under the porch of the Church [the Jews who will accept the Antichrist – John 5:43]. *All these things caused me much distress."*

October 1, 1820

"The Church is in great danger. We must pray so that the Pope may not leave Rome; countless evils would result if he did. They are now demanding something from him. The Protestant doctrine and that of the schismatic Greeks are to spread everywhere. I now see that in this place (Rome) the (Catholic) Church is being so cleverly undermined, that there hardly remain a hundred or so priests who have not been deceived. They all work for destruction, even the clergy. A great devastation is now near at hand."

In those days Faith will fall very low and it will be preserved in some places only.

The Little Black Man in Rome, whom I see so often, has many working for him without their clearly knowing for what end. He has his agents in the New Black Church also. If the Pope leaves Rome, the enemies of the Church will get the upper hand. I see the Little Black Man in his own country committing many thefts and falsifying things generally. Religion is there so skillfully undermined and stifled that there are scarcely 100 faithful priests. I cannot say how it is, but I see fog and darkness increasing ... All must be rebuilt soon; for everyone, even ecclesiastics, are laboring to destroy (and) ruin is at hand. The 2 enemies of the Church who have lost their accomplice are firmly resolved to destroy the pious and learned men that stand in their way..."

October 4, 1820

"When I saw the Church of St Peter in ruins and the manner in which so many of the clergy were themselves busy at this work of destruction – none of them wishing to do it openly in front of the

others – *I was in such distress that I cried out to Jesus with all my might, imploring His mercy. Then I saw before me the Heavenly Spouse, and He spoke to me for a long time...He said, among other things, that this translation of the Church from one place to another meant that she would seem to be in complete decline. But she would rise again; even if there remained but one Catholic, the Church would conquer again because she does not rest on human counsels and intelligence. It was shown to me that there were almost no Christians left in the old acceptation of the word."*

October 7, 1820

"As I was going through Rome with St. Francis and the other saint, we saw a great palace engulfed in flames from top to bottom. I was very much afraid that the occupants would be burned to death because no one came forward to put out the fire. As we came nearer, however, the fire abated and we saw the blackened building. We went through a number of magnificent rooms (untouched by the fire), and we finally reached the Pope. He was sitting in the dark and slept in a large arm-chair. He was very ill and weak; he could no longer walk. The ecclesiastics in the inner circle looked insincere and lacking in zeal; I did not like them. I told the Pope of the bishops who are to be appointed soon. I told him also that he must not leave Rome. If he did so, it would be chaos. He thought that the evil was inevitable and that he should leave in order to save many things beside himself. He was very much inclined to leave Rome, and he was insistently urged to do so. The Pope is still attached to the things of this earth in many ways..."

"The Church is completely isolated and as if completely deserted. It seems that everyone is running away. Everywhere I see great misery, hatred, treason, rancor, confusion and utter blindness. O city! O city! What is threatening thee? The storm is coming, do be watchful...!"

June 1, 1821

"Among the strangest things that I saw, were long processions of bishops. Their thoughts and utterances were made known to me through images issuing from their mouths. Their faults towards religion were shown by external deformities. A few had only a body, with a dark cloud of fog instead of a head. Others had only a head, their bodies and hearts were like thick vapors. Some were lame; others were paralytics; others were asleep or staggering. I saw what I believe to be nearly all the bishops of the world, but only a small number were perfectly sound. I also saw the Holy Father – God-fearing and prayerful. Nothing left to be desired in his appearance, but he was weakened by old age and by much suffering. His head was lolling from side to side, and it dropped onto his chest as if he was falling asleep. He often fainted and seemed to be dying. But when he was praying, he was often comforted by apparitions from Heaven. Then, his head was erect, but as soon as it dropped again onto his chest, I saw a number of people looking quickly right and left, that is, in the direction of the world..."

"Then I saw that everything pertaining to Protestantism was gradually gaining the upper hand, and the Catholic religion fell into complete decadence. Most priests were lured by the glittering but false knowledge of young school-teachers, and they all contributed to the work of destruction. In those days, Faith will fall very low, and it will be preserved in some places only, in a few cottages and in a few families which God has protected from disasters and wars..."

1820-1821

"I also saw the various regions of the earth. My Guide (Jesus) named Europe and pointing to a small and sandy region, He uttered these words: 'Here is Prussia (East Germany), the enemy.' Then He showed me another place, to the north, and He said: 'This is Moskva, the land of Moscow, bringing many evils."

"*I see many excommunicated ecclesiastics who do not seem to be concerned about it, nor even aware of it. Yet, they are (ipso factor) excommunicated whenever they cooperated to [sic] enterprises, enter into associations, and embrace opinions on which an anathema has been cast* [i.e., become Freemasons]. *It can be seen thereby that God ratifies the decrees, orders, and interdictions issued by the Head of the Church, and that He keeps them in force even though men show no concern for them, reject them, or laugh them to scorn.*"

April 22, 1823

"*I saw that many pastors allowed themselves to be taken up with ideas that were dangerous to the Church. They were building a great, strange, and extravagant Church. Everyone was to be admitted in it in order to be united and have equal rights: Evangelicals, Catholics sects of every description. Such was to be the new Church...But God had other designs...*"

"*I see that when the Second Coming of Christ approaches, a bad priest will do much harm to the Church. When the time of the reign of Antichrist is near, a false religion will appear which will be opposed to the unity of God and His Church. This will cause the greatest schism the world has ever known. The nearer the time of the end, the more the darkness of Satan will spread on earth, the greater will be the number of the children of corruption, and the number of the just will correspondingly diminish...*

They built a large, singular, extravagant church which was to embrace all creeds with equal rights: Evangelicals, Catholics, and all denominations, a true communion of the unholy with one shepherd and one flock. There was to be a Pope, a salaried Pope, without possessions. All was made ready, many things finished; but, in place of an altar, were only abomination and desolation. Such was the new church to be, and it was for it that he had set fire to the old one; but God designed otherwise...."

I came to the Church of Peter and Paul (Rome) and saw a dark world of distress, confusion, and corruption, through which shone countless graces from thousands of saints who there repose...

I saw the fatal consequences of this counterfeit church: I saw it increase; I saw heretics of all kinds flocking to the city. I saw the ever-increasing tepidity of the clergy, the circle of darkness ever widening...

Again, I saw in the midst of these disasters the twelve new Apostles laboring in different countries, unknown to one another, each receiving streams of living water from on high They all did the same work. They know not whence they received their tasks; but as soon as one was finished, another was ready for them..."

"The Jews shall return to Palestine, and become Christians toward the end of the world."

October 22, 1822

"Very bad times will come when non-Catholics will lead many people astray. A great confusion will result. I saw the battle also. The enemies were far more numerous, but the small army of the faithful cut down whole rows of enemy soldiers. During the battle, the Blessed Virgin stood on a hill, wearing a suit armor. It was a terrible war. At the end, only a few fighters for the just cause survived, but the victory was theirs..."

CHAPTER 27

St. Francis of Assisi

Francis of Assisi (born **Giovanni di Pietro di Bernardone;** *Italian*: Francesco d'Assisi; *Latin*: Franciscus Assisiensis; 1181 or 1182 – 3 October 1226) is venerated as Saint Francis of Assisi, also known in his ministry as Francesco, was an Italian Catholic friar, deacon, mystic and preacher. He founded the men's Order of Friars Minor, the women's Order of Saint Clare, the Third Order of Saint Francis and the Custody of the Holy Land. He is one of the most venerated religious figures in Christianity.

Pope Gregory IX canonized Francis on July 16, 1228. He was designated patron saint of Italy along with Saint Catherine of Siena. He later became associated with patronage of animals and the natural environment. It then became customary for churches to hold ceremonies blessing animals on or near his feast day of October 4. In 1219, he went to Egypt in an attempt to convert the Sultan to put an end to the conflict of the Crusades. By this time, the Franciscan Order had grown to a level that its primitive organizational structure was no longer sufficient. He then returned to Italy to organize the Order. Once his community was authorized by the Pope, he withdrew increasingly from external affairs.

Francis is known for his love of the Eucharist. In 1223, he arranged for the first Christmas live nativity scene. According to Christian tradition, in 1224, he received the stigmata during the apparition of Seraphic angels in a religious ecstasy. This would make him the second person in Christian tradition after St. Paul (Galatians 6:17) to bear the wounds of Christ's Passion. He died during the evening hours of October 3, 1226. He was listening to a reading he had requested of Psalm 142.

St. Francis' Early life

Francis was born in late 1181 or early 1182. He was one of several children of an Italian father, Pietro di Bernardone dei Mariconi and a French mother, Pica de Bourlemont. Pietro was a prosperous silk merchant while little is known about Pica except that she was a noblewoman originally from Provence. Pietro was in France on business when Francis was born in Assisi. Pica had him baptized as Giovanni. Upon his return to Assisi, Pietro took to calling his son Francesco ('the Frenchman") possibly in honor of his commercial success and enthusiasm for all things French. Since the child was renamed in infancy, the change would have hardly to do with his aptitude for learning French, as some would have surmised.

Indulged by his parents, Francis lived the high-spirited life of a wealthy young man. He was handsome, witty, gallant and delighted in fine clothes. He spent money lavishly. Although many hagiographers commented about his bright clothing, rich friends and love of pleasures, his display of disillusionment toward the world that surrounded him came fairly early in his life. Such is shown in the "story of the beggar." In this account, he was selling cloth and velvet in the marketplace on behalf of his father when a beggar approached him and asked for alms. At the conclusion of the conversation, Francis abandoned his wares and ran after the beggar. When he found him, Francis gave the man everything he had in his pockets. His friends quickly rebuked and mocked him for his act of charity. When he got home, his father scolded him in rage.

Around 1202, he joined a military expedition against Perugia and was taken as a prisoner at Collestrada. He spent a year as a captive and an illness caused him to reevaluate his life. It is possible that his spiritual conversion, which could have been a gradual process, was rooted in this experience. When he returned to Assisi in 1203, Francis returned to his carefree life. In 1205, Francis left for Apulia to enlist in the army of Walter III, Count of Brienne. A strange vision made him return to Assisi, having lost his taste for the worldly life. Based on hagiographic accounts, he thereby began to avoid the sports and the feasts of his former companions. In response, they asked him mockingly whether he was thinking of marrying to which he answered, "Yes, a fairer bride than any of you have ever seen," meaning his "Lady Poverty."

On a pilgrimage to Rome, he joined the indigent in begging at St. Peter's Basilica. He spent some time in outcast places as he was asking God for spiritual enlightenment. He said he had a mystical vision of Jesus Christ in the abandoned country chapel of San Damiano, just outside of Assisi. The icon of Christ Crucified said to him, "Francis, Francis, go and repair My house which, as you can see, is falling into ruins." He took this to refer to the ruined church in which he was presently praying. He then sold some cloth from his father's store to assist the priest there for this objective. When the priest refused to accept the ill-gotten gains, an aggrieved Francis threw the coins on the floor.

In order to avoid his father's wrath, Francis hid in a cave near San Damiano for about a month. When he returned to town, he was hungry and dirty. He was dragged home by his father, beaten, bound and locked in a small storeroom. Freed by his mother during his father's absence, Francis returned at once to San Damiano. He found shelter with the officiating priest. He was however soon cited before the city consuls by his father.

Not content with having recovered the scattered gold from San Damiano, Bernardone also sought to force his son to forego his inheritance, by way of restitution. In the midst of legal proceedings before the Bishop of Assisi, Francis renounced his father and his patrimony. Some accounts report that he stripped himself naked in the token of this renunciation. The Bishop covered him with his own cloak.

For the next couple of months, Francis roamed around as a beggar in the hills behind Assisi. For some time, he also worked as a scullion at a neighboring monastery. He then went to Gubbio, where as alms, a friend gave him a cloak, a girdle and staff of a pilgrim. He returned to Assisi, traversing the city begging stones for the restoration of St. Damiano's. He carried these stones to the old chapel, set in place himself and so at length rebuilt it. Over the course of two years, he embraced the life of a penitent, during which he restored several ruined chapels in the countryside around Assisi.

Founding of The Friars Minor

In a morning of February 1208, Francis was participating in a Mass in the chapel of St. Mary of the Angels, near which he had then built himself a hut. The Gospel of the day was from the book of Matthew, the "Commissioning of the Twelve." The disciples are to go and proclaim the Kingdom of God is at hand. Francis was inspired to devote himself to a life of poverty. Having obtained a coarse woolen tunic, he tied it around him with a knotted rope. It was the clothing of the poorest Umbrian peasants. He then immediately went forth and at once exhorted people of the countryside to penance, brotherly love and peace. Francis' preaching to ordinary people was uncommon since he had no license to do so. His example drew others to him such that within a year, Francis had eleven followers. The brothers lived a simple life in the deserted lazar house of Rivo Torto near Assisi but they spent much of their time meandering through the mountainous districts of Umbria, making a deep impression upon their hearers by their intense exhortations.

In 1209, Francis composed a simple rule for his followers ("friars"), the *Regula Primitiva* or "Primitive Rule." It came from verses in the Bible. The rule was to follow the teachings of our Lord Jesus Christ and to walk in his footsteps." He then took his first eleven followers to Rome to seek permission from Pope Innocent III to found a new religious Order. Upon entry to Rome, the brothers met Bishop Guido of Assisi, who was with Giovanni di San Paolo, the Cardinal Bishop of Sabina, confessor of Pope Innocent III. The Cardinal was immediately sympathetic to Francis and agreed to represent Francis to the pope. Pope Innocent III, reluctantly agreed to meet with Francis and the brothers the next day. It was after several days that the pope agreed to admit the group informally, adding that when God increased the group in grace and number, they could return for an official admittance. The group was tonsured. This was important because it recognized Church authority and prevented his following from possible accusations of heresy. Though a number of the Pope's counselors considered the mode of life proposed by Francis as unsafe and impractical, he decided to endorse Francis' order because of a dream he had. He dreamt that Francis was holding up the Basilica of St. John Lateran (the cathedral of Rome, thus the 'home church' of all Christendom). Thus, according to tradition, on April 16, 1210, the official founding of the Franciscan Order was constituted. The group, then the "Lesser Brothers" (Order of Friars Minor also known as the Franciscan Order or the Seraphic Order) were centered in the Porziuncola and preached first in Umbria before they expanded throughout Italy. Francis chose never to be ordained a priest, although he was later ordained as a deacon.

From then on, the new Order grew fast with new vocations. Hearing Francis preaching in the church of San Rufino in Assisi in 1211, the young noblewoman, Clare of Assisi became deeply touched by his message and understood her calling. Her cousin Rufino, the only male member of the family in their generation, was also attracted to the new Order, which he later joined. On the night of Palm Sunday, March 28,1212, Clare covertly left her family's palace. Francis received her at the Porziuncola and thereby established the Order of Poor Ladies, an order for women. Francis gave Clare a religious habit, or garment, similar to his own, before lodging her in a nearby monastery of Benedictine nuns until he could find a suitable retreat for her and her younger sister, Caterina and the other young women who had joined her. Later, he transferred them to San Damiano, to a few small huts or cells of wattle, straw and mud, enclosed by a hedge. This became the first monastery of the Second Franciscan Order, now known as Poor Clares.

For those who could not leave their homes, he later formed the Third Order of Brothers and Sisters of Penance, a fraternity composed of either laity or clergy. Its members neither withdrew from the world nor took religious vows and instead observed the principles of Franciscan life in their daily lives. Before long, this Third Order grew beyond Italy. The Third Order is now titled the Secular Franciscan Order.

Determined to bring the Gospel to everyone in the world and convert them, after the example of the first disciples of Jesus, Francis sought on several occasions to take his message out of Italy. In the late spring of 1212, he set out for Jerusalem but was shipwrecked by a storm on the Dalmatian coast. It forced him to return to Italy. In the same year, Francis sailed for Morocco, but this time an illness forced him to break off his journey in Spain. Back in Assisi, several noblemen, among them Tommaso de Celano (who would later write the biography of St. Francis), and some well-educated men joined his Order. In 1215, it wasn't for certain but Francis may have gone to Rome for the Fourth Lateran Council. It would be around this time that he probably met a canon, Dominic de Guzman, (later to be Saint Dominic, the founder of the Friars Preacher, another Catholic religious order.) In 1217, he offered to go to France but Cardinal Ugolino of Segni (the future Pope Gregory IX), advised him against this and said that he was still needed in Italy.

Travels

In 1219, Francis went to Egypt during the Fifth Crusade. He was accompanied by another friar and was hoping to convert the Sultan of Egypt or win martyrdom in the process. A Crusader army had encamped for over a year besieging the walled city of Damietta, two miles upstream from one of the main channels of the Nile. The Sultan, al-Kamil, a nephew of Saladin, had succeeded his father as Sultan of Egypt in 1218 and was unable to relieve being encamped upstream of Damietta. A bloody and futile attack on the city was launched by the Christians on August 29, 1210, following which both sides agreed to a ceasefire. The ceasefire lasted about four weeks and was probably the interlude when Francis and his companions crossed the Muslims' lines and were brought before the Sultan, remaining in his camp for a few days. There was no information about what transpired. No contemporary Arab sources mentioned the visit either. One detail, however was added by Bonaventure in the biography of St. Francis written forty years after the event. It was said that Francis offered to challenge the Sultan's "priests" with trial-by-fire in order to prove the veracity of the Christian Gospel.

Such an incident is alluded to in a late 13th century fresco scene attributed to Giotto, in the upper basilica at Assisi. Although Bonaventure asserts that the Sultan refused to allow the challenge, subsequent biographies went further, claiming that a fire was actually kindled. Francis unhesitatingly entered the fire without getting burnt. Many scholars have expressed their doubts that Giotto was the author of the Upper Church frescoes.

According to some late sources, the Sultan allowed Francis to visit the sacred places in the Holy Land and even to preach there. All that can be safely presumed is that Francis and his companion left the Crusader camp from Acre, from where they left for Italy in the latter half of 1220. Based on a 1267 sermon by Bonaventure, later sources report that the Sultan discreetly converted or accepted a death-bed baptism as a result of the encounter with Francis. The Franciscan Order has been present in the Holy Land almost uninterruptedly since 1217. It received concessions from the Mameluke Sultan in 1333 with regard to certain Holy Places in Jerusalem and Bethlehem, and (so far as concerns the Catholic Church) jurisdictional privileges from Pope Clement VI in 1342.

Reorganization of the Franciscan Order

By this time, the growing Order of friars was divided into provinces. Groups were sent to France, Germany, Hungary and Spain to the East. Francis returned to Italy via Venice upon hearing the report of the martyrdom of five brothers in Morocco. Another reason for Francis' return to Italy was that the Franciscan Order had grown at an unprecedented rate compared to previous religious orders. Its organizational sophistication, however, had not kept up with its growth and needed a little more than Francis' example and simple rule. Francis then prepared a new and more detailed Rule, the "First Rule" or "Rule Without a Papal Bull" (Regula prima, regula non bullata). The rule asserted devotion to poverty and the apostolic life. However, it also introduced greater institutional structure, though never officially endorsed by the pope. He later created the Second Rule or "Rule with a Bull" which was approved by Pope Honorius on November 29, 1223. It called the friars "to observe the Holy Gospel of our Lord Jesus Christ, living in obedience without anything of our own and in chastity." In addition, it set guidelines for discipline, preaching and entry into the Order. Once the Rule was validated by the Pope, Francis withdrew increasingly from external affairs. During 1221 and 1222, Francis crossed Italy, first as far south as Catania in Sicily and as far north as Bologna.

Stigmata, Final Days, and Sainthood

On or about September 13, 1224, the Feast of the Exaltation of the Cross, Francis is said to have a vision of a seraph, a six-winged angel on a cross. The angel gave him the gift of the five wounds of Christ. Suffering from the stigmata and from trachoma, Francis received care in several cities (Siena, Cortona, Nocera) to no avail. In the end, he was brought back to a hut next to the Porziuncola. Back to the place where the Franciscan movement began, feeling that his end was near, Francis spent his final days dictating his spiritual testament. He died on the evening of Saturday, October 3, 1226, singing Psalm 141, "Voce mea ad Dominum." Two years later, on July 16, 1228, Francis was pronounced a saint by Pope Gregory IX (the former cardinal Ugolino di Conti, a friend of St. Francis and Cardinal Protector of the Order. The next day, the Pope laid the foundation stone for the Basilica of Saint Francis in Assisi. Francis was buried on May 25, 1230, under the Lower Basilica but his tomb was hidden to protect it from Saracen invaders. His exact burial place remained unknown until it was rediscovered in 1818. Pasquale Belli then constructed for the remains a crypt in the neo-classical style in the Lower Basilica. It was refashioned between 1927 and 1930 into its present form by Ugo Tarchi. Marble decorations were stripped from the wall. In 1978, the remains of St. Francis were examined and confirmed by a commission of scholars appointed by Pope Paul VI. The remains were put into a glass urn in the ancient stone tomb.

It has become a popular practice on his feastday, October 4, for people to bring their pets and other animals to a church for a blessing.

Feast day

"A man, not canonically elected, will be raised to the Pontificate... In those days Jesus Christ will send them not a true Pastor, but a Destroyer"

It would have been around May 15, 2021 that Pope Francis exhorted in his Mass "Keeping the Truth does not mean defending ideas, becoming guardians of a system of doctrines and dogmas. It is remaining bound to Christ and by being devoted to His Gospel. Truth is Christ Himself."

Social media evangelist Dr. Taylor Marshall considered this statement a bifurcation of the faith. It means that the faith is dived into two parts or two branches which oppose what St. Paul and early theologians have said about guarding the deposit of the faith.

Pope Francis may have taken his cue from when the St. Damiano's crucifix spoke to St. Francis. "Francis, Francis, repair my House..." However, Pope Francis' plenty of responses have been deemed heretical by a good portion of the Catholic Church.

Shortly before his death in 1226, St. Francis of Assisi called together the member of his order and warned them of great tribulations that would befall the Church in the future, saying:

"Act bravely, my Brethren; take courage and trust in the Lord. The time is fast approaching in which there will be great trials and afflictions; perplexities and dissensions, both spiritual and temporal, will abound; the charity of many will grow cold, and the malice of the wicked will increase.

The devils will have unusual power, the immaculate purity of our Order, and of others, will be so much obscured that there will be very few Christians who will obey the true Sovereign Pontiff and the Roman Church with loyal hearts and perfect charity. At the time of this tribulation a man, not canonically elected, will be raised to the Pontificate, who, by his cunning, will endeavor to draw many into error and death. Then scandals will be multiplied, our Order will be divided, and many others will be entirely destroyed, because they will consent to error instead of opposing it.

There will be such diversity of opinions and schisms among the people, the religious and the clergy, that, except those days were shortened, according to the words of the Gospel, even the elect would be led into error, were they not specially guided, amid such great confusion, by the immense mercy of God. Then our Rule and manner of life will be violently opposed by some, and terrible trials will come upon us. Those who are found faithful will receive the crown of life; but woe to those who, trusting solely in their Order, shall fall into tepidity, for they will not be able to support the temptations permitted for the proving of the elect.

Those who preserve their fervor and adhere to virtue with love and zeal for the truth, will suffer injuries and, persecutions as rebels and schismatics; for their persecutors, urged on by the evil spirits, will say they are rendering a great service to God by destroying such pestilent men from the face of the earth. But the Lord will be the refuge of the afflicted, and will save all who trust in Him. And in order to be like their Head [Jesus Christ], these, the elect, will act with confidence, and by their death will purchase for themselves eternal life; choosing to obey God rather than man, they will fear nothing, and they will prefer to perish [physically] rather than consent to falsehood and perfidy.

Some preachers will keep silence about the truth, and others will trample it underfoot and deny it. Sanctity of life will be held in derision even by those who outwardly profess it, for in those days Jesus Christ will send them not a true Pastor, but a destroyer."

Clearly, these prophetic words of St. Francis have never been more relevant than today. It has been rumored that St. Francis also said that the false pope he was warning against would take his own name ("Francis"), but this information has not been verified nor a source found for it.

Some people dispute the authenticity of this prophecy, claiming it was concocted by certain dissident members of the Franciscan order in the 13th century and only subsequently attributed to St. Francis. Whether that be true or false, always keep in mind that ultimately, the case against the Vatican II antipopes is not based on private revelation.

Pope Benedict XVI's resignation from papacy is still quite unclear. Some interpret it as he resigned from the Petrine office but not from the Petrine ministry. Thereby, he is still technically a pope which puts the election of Pope Francis under some questionable authority. It is of no doubt that Pope Francis has the Petrine office but does he share the Petrine ministry with Pope Benedict XVI? There seems to be canonical question.

CHAPTER 28

"Build Me A Church"

It was actually the summer of 2014. I attended the "Risk Jesus 2014." It was a gathering of singers, composers and reflective authors. It was something sort of funny that Fr. Dwight, one of the speakers was talking about the letter of St. Paul was not meant for the "Philippinos." He looked at me and then suddenly people started looking at me. I was like, "What??" There were five other pews of people and people started looking over other people to look at me.

After that was a breaktime, I was actually waiting for Fr.Dwight to get over with whatever he was doing but he was answering questions from people who had been checking out his publications. As I was waiting, I was talking to somebody about some future plans. It was then a husband and wife interrupted me and gave me contact information about the Marian Catechists. The Marian Catechists is a formational program designed by Fr. John Hardon SJ. It was in reply to a request of St. John Paul 2.

I was able to talk to Fr. Dwight briefly. I did later call the Marian Catechists and they sent me a whole package to learn about the Catechism of the Catholic Church together with some formation program. A few months later, I received a letter regarding building a Shrine for Our Lady of Guadalupe, signed by Raymond Cardinal

Burke. That is how I became familiar with Cardinal Burke who had become the lead in opposing Pope Francis in many of his heretical ways.

I was actually able to visit the St. John Paul 2 Shrine which also had Our Lady of Guadalupe.

"**Our Lady of Guadalupe**, Spanish **Nuestra Señora de Guadalupe**, also called **the Virgin of Guadalupe,** in Roman Catholicism, the Virgin Mary in her appearance before St. Juan Diego in a vision in 1531. The name also refers to the Marian apparition itself. Our Lady of Guadalupe holds a special place in the religious life of Mexico and is one of the most popular religious devotions. Her image has played an important role as a national symbol of Mexico.

According to tradition, Mary appeared to Juan Diego, who was an Aztec convert to Christianity on December 9 and again on December 12, 1531. She requested that a shrine to her be built on the spot where she appeared, Tepeyac Hill (now in a suburb of Mexico City. The bishop demanded a sign before he would approve construction of a church, however. Mary appeared a second time to Juan Diego and ordered him to collect roses. In a second audience with the bishop, Juan Diego opened his cloak, letting dozens of roses fall to the floor and revealing the image of Mary imprinted on the inside of the cloak—the image that is now venerated in the Basilica of Guadalupe.

The traditional view has been questioned by various scholars and ecclesiastics, including the former abbot of the Basilica of Guadalupe. The primary objection is that there is no documentary evidence for the apparition until 1648; critics claim that documents purporting to be from the 16th century are actually from the 17th. Critics have also noted that the bishop approached by Juan Diego was not consecrated until 1534, and he makes no mention of Juan Diego or of Our Lady of Guadalupe in his writings. Defenders of the Virgin of Guadalupe—including Pope John Paul II who canonized Juan Diego and declared Our Lady of Guadalupe the patroness of the Americas—accept the authenticity of the early documents and point also to various oral accounts of the apparition."

I don't believe the apparition and its meaning ended there. There was a time when Mama and I got involved in building a Church back at home. The old chapel was replaced with a new parish, Church building. However, I believe Mary is talking about rebuilding of the Catholic faith.

CONCLUSION

I believe I have laid out my own experiences of Mary and I have laid out what most saints said about their apocalyptic predictions. Going back to the very first chapter where it says:

"In its comprehension of the strict sense, it means the foreknowledge of future events, though it may sometimes apply to past events of which there is no memory, and to present hidden things which cannot be known by the natural light of reason."

I once talked about how I got reminded of the Jewish times when I saw the pastor frequently doing handwashing as required in dealing with the coronavirus pandemic. I did pull up information and it said that "water is poured from a vessel three times in preparation for a blessing or reading of the Torah…" It just clicked in me. Something kind of triggered an old, stored memory.

I remember at one point I was warning the Church authorities about a new viral strain, out of my interpretation of the message of La Salette. I was looking at several sexually transmitted diseases including hepatitis of which a new strain might develop. It actually developed from the SARS. They were pandemics of which have not had been resolved yet. Coronavirus was a new viral strain said to have been developed in a Chinese lab as a biochemical weapon, although that still has to be proven. I later warned them about New York being hit by something like a bomb. That was in 2019. In 2020, New York became the epicenter of the coronavirus pandemic in the United States. The staggering numbers of those needing intensive care units with ventilators were staggering. It happened not only once but twice. I also prophesied about the asymptomatics of the coronavirus. At one point, plenty of those infected were asymptomatic.

At one point, I believe I may have saved the US from the North Korea bomb. North Korea gave a certain date as to when it will bomb Hawaii. I sat on my computer just writing down my thoughts. Since North Korea had been experimenting on ground missiles, no one had thought of underwater attacks. I gave notice to the government authorities that they might be firing missiles from submarines or under the water. The day of threat came and North Korea rescinded on their threat. I believe they actually rescinded a few days earlier but wasn't definite about it.

In another story, like St. Malachy, I saw at one point inside the Basilica of St. Peter in Rome, a list of the popes throughout history. It was displayed near a confessional box almost in the middle of the Church. I thought I took a picture. Apparently, I did not take a picture although I did notice it. I took a picture instead of something about St. John Paul 2 who was the Pope at that time.

Like St. Francis, I saw a tree once, all filled with birds. I was just coming out from St. Lucy's Church and I heard something abuzz with birds so I looked for it. There was a tree where the birds looked like its leaves. Plenty left the tree and it was such a sight to see but I think plenty was left in the tree. The tree was quite a distance from me. I thought it was something magical. I thought that there is somewhere I read about it but I cannot remember then.

Many of the stories that surround the life of Saint Francis say that he had a great love for animals and the environment. The "Fioretti" ("Little Flowers"), is a collection of legends and folklore that sprang up after the Saint's death. One account describes how one day, while Francis was traveling with some companions, they happened upon a place in the road where birds filled the trees on either side. Francis told his companions to "wait for me while I go to preach to my sisters the birds." The birds surrounded him, intrigued by the power of his voice, and not one of them flew away. He is often portrayed with a bird, typically in his hand.

My vision was also like that of Anna Catherine of Emmerich where she was in the scene but people could not see her and she had Jesus as her guide throughout that mystical experience.

I talked about when I saw the world war scenes shown to me by Mary, I was in the scene but people could not see me. I was like part of that movie frame but invisible to them. Jesus was also my Guide when I visited hell and purgatory.

The visions and the prophecies offered some variety of endings. St. Malachy said that Petrus Romanus is the last pope. Does that mean end of the Catholic Church or end of the world because Jesus is supposed to come back as the Judge? If Jesus is to reveal Himself, back in the world, that means Final Judgment.

What is interesting for me was that I seem to have had the continuation of the vision of Anna Katherine of Emmerich:

There they me a Woman of noble carriage who seemed to be with child because she walked slowly. At this sight, the enemies were terrorized and the Beast could not take another step forward. It projected its neck towards the Woman as if to devour her, but the Woman turned about and bowed down (towards the altar), her head touching the ground. Thereupon, I saw the Beast taking to flight towards the sea again, and the enemies were fleeing in the greatest confusion....Then, I saw in the great distance great legion approaching. In the foreground, I saw a man on a white horse. Prisoners were set free and joined them. All enemies were pursued. Then, I saw that the Church was being promptly rebuilt and she was more magnificent than ever before..."

There was a ship with a dragon's head as its masthead. It lunged at me three times trying to attack me but I did not even flinch because I knew it was powerless over me. The next thing I knew was that I was inside a jail. My head was bowed down that when the anti-Christ arrived by the jail door on my left, I only saw his boots. His boots looked nice. He seems to be of sophisticated standing, a highly educated person. I knew he was the anti-Christ. He told me, "It's you!!!" Knowing that he was powerless over me, he said, "I will come back for you later" and left.

"In the foreground, I saw a man on a white horse. Prisoners were set free and joined them. All enemies were pursued. Then, I saw that the Church was being promptly rebuilt and she was more magnificent than ever before..."

A man on a white horse is understood to be the person of Jesus Christ riding a white horse, meaning conquest. It can also mean the anti-Christ but in the context of Emmerich's prophecy, it sounds more like Jesus Christ.

And the Church was rebuilt magnificently. Is this an earthly kingdom or a heavenly kingdom?

I myself would rather not see apocalyptic scenes. I requested that I do not see apocalyptic scenes. It remains that God the Father is the only One who knows about whether these are the end of times or not. It was prophesied that after pastoring the sheep through tumultuous times by Petrus Romanus, Rome will be destroyed. It was also prophesied in Revelation, Chapter 17, that "the city of seven hills where the prostitute Babylon sits will be destroyed." I have to pray that I receive the key to this but even if I do, I would rather not see the destruction of Rome.

I would rather say, hopefully there's a nice surprise at the end.

In Revelation comes the fulfillment of a wedding banquet, which is the ultimate metaphor in Christian theology. Christ is regarded as the Bridegroom and there's a Bride waiting. In Revelation, this becomes a reality when Christ comes back. We all know that the Bible combines reality with figures of speech, oftentimes prophecies are alluded to by certain realities. I want to say I am waiting for this to happen.

Could it be that St. John Paul 2 gave us a clue to a new era? He included the flowering staff of St. Joseph in the chapel of St. John

Paul 2 Center. It opens the door to the monastic, gnostic, esoteric understanding of the revelations of Christ.

The question really is about Pope Francis. His heritage has Italian ties, therefore "Romanus." His parents emigrated from Italy to Argentina early on for a better life. St. Hildegard's quote that the anti-Christ advocates for "do as you please" seem synonymous with Francis' "be messy." Anna Katherine Emmerich's vision of the pope living somewhere else and of the idolatry and emptiness of the Vatican that she saw seems to portend what else was in her prophecy. St. Francis' prophecy of a pope not canonically elected seems to also hint at the situation that Pope Francis have. The Vatican went through legitimate means of electing him, it is just that a situation hangs in the context of his election.

It's kind of hard to believe that Time will end. But I believe people are allowed to live as if life will go on. As Jesus said let the good be good and bad be bad until such time when the chaff is separated from the wheat.

REFERENCES

"Amoris Letitia." Wikipedia. Retrieved from https://en.wikipedia.org/wiki/Amoris_laetitia. March 30, 2021.

"Anne Catherine of Emmerich" Wikipedia. Retrieved from https://en.wikipedia.org/wiki/Anne_Catherine_Emmerich, May 21, 2021.

"Apparition of the Blessed Virgin Mary on the Mountain La Salette, on the 19th of September, 1846, The Pope in Red. Retrieved from http://www.thepopeinred.com/secret.htm, March 29, 2021.

Apparitions Statistics, Modern. Marian Apparitions of the 20th and 21st Centuries. A Directory of 20th and 21st century Apparition through 2011. University of Dayton. Retrieved from https://udayton.edu/imri/mary/a/apparitions-statistics-modern.php#:~:text=A%20statistical%20analysis%20of%20the,299%20of%20the%20386%20cases. May 17, 2021.

"Attorney General Kamala Harris turns down Prop 8 defense before Supreme Court" ABC7.com. Retrieved from https://abc7.com/archive/9042429/. April 6, 2021.

"Blessed Anne Catherine Emmerich's Prophecy on Two Popes" These Last Days News, June 9, 2016. Retrieved from https://www.tldm.org/news29/blessed-anne-catherine-emmerichs-prophecy-on-two-popes.htm. May 18, 2021.

"Covid-19 US Cases by County" Johns Hopkins University. Retrieved from https://coronavirus.jhu.edu/us-map. April 4, 2021.

"Covid-19 Lockdowns" Wikipedia. Retrieved from https://en.wikipedia.org/wiki/COVID-19_lockdowns, March 25, 2021

"Fatima: A Mystery Explained?" FSSPX News. Retrieved from https://fsspx.news/en/news-events/news/fatima-mystery-explained-41275. April 7, 2021.

"Four Messages from Our Lady of Garabandal" Garabandal.org. Retrieved from http://www.garabandal.org/News/Message_7.shtml. April 6, 2021

"Francis of Assisi" Wikipedia. Retrieved from https://en.wikipedia.org/wiki/Francis_of_Assisi. May 21, 2021.

"God's Chat with the Devil" Catholic Stand, May 18, 2018 issue, Retrieved from https://catholicstand.com/gods-chat-devil-popeleo/, March 31, 2021.

Good News Bible. American Society, New York, 1976.

"Has Pope Leo XIII's 100-Year Vision Reached its Terminus?" The Five Beasts. "The Message of Fatima" Congregation for the Doctrine of the Faith. Retrieved from https://www.vatican.va/roman_curia/congregations/cfaith/documents/rc_con_cfaith_doc_20000626_message-fatima_en.html. April 6, 2021

"Hildegard of Bingen" Wikipedia. Retrieved from https://en.wikipedia.org/wiki/Hildegard_of_Bingen, May 21, 2021.

"Italy Earthquake 2016" Geography.org. Retrieved from https://www.geography.org.uk/teaching-resources/earthquakes-tsunamis/italy-2016. March 26, 2021.

"List of George Floyd protests in the United States" Wikipedia. Retrieved from https://en.wikipedia.org/wiki/List_of_George_Floyd_protests_in_the_United_States. March 25, 2021.

"The Impact of Coronavirus in Food Insecurity in 2020 and 2021." Feeding America.org Retrieved from https://www.feedingamerica.org/

sites/default/files/2021-03/National%20Projections%20Brief_3.9.2021 0.pdf. March 26, 2021.

John de Marchi, LMC. "The True Story of Fatima. A Complete Account of Fatima Apparitions." The Fatima Center. New York.

Lindsay Schnell. "Most priests accused of sexually abusing children were never sent to prison. Here's why." Retrieved from USA Today. https://www.usatoday.com/story/news/nation/2019/11/11/catholic-sex-abuse-why-dont-accused-priests-go-jail/3997022002/ March 29, 2021.

Michael Joseph Gross. "The Vatican's Secret Life" December 2013. Vanity Fair. Retrieved from https://www.vanityfair.com/culture/2013/12/gay-clergy-catholic-church-vatican. May 17, 2021.

"Report Reveals Widespread Sexual Abuse by Over 300 Priests in Pennsylvania" Retrieved from NPR. https://www.npr.org/2018/08/18/639698062/the-clergy-abuse-crisis-has-cost-the-catholic-church-3-billion, March 29, 2021.

"Same-sex Marriage" Wikipedia. Retrieved from https://en.wikipedia.org/wiki/Same-sex_marriage. April 5, 2021.

"The Message of Fatima" Congregation for the Doctrine of the Faith. Retrieved from https://www.vatican.va/roman_curia/congregations/cfaith/documents/rc_con_cfaith_doc_20000626_message-fatima_en.html. April 6, 2021.

"30th Anniversary of John Paul II's Assassination Attempt" Retrieved from YouTube Rome Reports.com, April 9, 2021

"The Pope in Red" The Pope in Red. Retrieved from http://www.thepopeinred.com/secret.htm. March 26, 2021.

"Obergefell v Hodges" Wikipedia. Retrieved from https://en.wikipedia.org/wiki/Obergefell_v._Hodges. April 5, 2021.

"Our Lady of Akita." Retrieved from Wikipedia. https://en.wikipedia.org/wiki/Our_Lady_of_Akita. April 19, 2021.

"Our Lady of Kazan" Wikipedia. Retrieved from https://en.wikipedia.org/wiki/Our_Lady_of_Kazan, May 12, 2021.

"Pachamama Is A Demon: Testimony from A Missionary" Joshua Charles. Retrieved from https://www.joshuatcharles.com/blog/2020/4/24/pachamama-is-a-demon-testimony-from-missionaries. May 19, 2021.

"Pope Benedict XVI. Wikipedia. Retrieved from https://en.wikipedia.org/wiki/Pope_Benedict_XVI. May 5, 2021.

"Pope John Paul II" Retrieved from Wikipedia. https://en.wikipedia.org/wiki/Pope_John_Paul_II. April 6, 2021.

"Prophecy." Catholic.com. Retrieved from https://www.catholic.com/encyclopedia/prophecy. May 17, 2021.

"Rome Catholic Churches ordered closed due to coronavirus, unprecedented in modern times"

Reuters. Retrieved from https://www.reuters.com/article/us-health-coronavirus-italy-rome-churche/rome-catholic-churches-ordered-closed-due-to-coronavirus-unprecedented-in-modern-times-idUSKBN20Z3BU. May 19, 2021.

"Russian Orthodox Church" New World Encyclopedia. Retrieved from https://www.newworldencyclopedia.org/entry/Russian_Orthodox_Church#:~:text=In%20the%20first%20five%20years,or%20sent%20to%20labor%20camps. April 6, 2021.

"Saint Malachy" Wikipedia. Retrieved from https://en.wikipedia.org/wiki/Saint_Malachy, May 21, 2021.

"Sobreiro Monumental" Wikipedia. Retrieved from https://en.wikipedia.org/wiki/Sobreiro_Monumental. April 7, 2021.

"Solar eclipse of August 21, 2017" Wikipedia. Retrieved from https://en.wikipedia.org/wiki/Solar_eclipse_of_August_21,_2017. May 21, 2021

"The Beginning". The Garabandal Story. Retrieved from http://www.garabandal.org/story.shtml May 5, 2021.

"Theological and Canonical Implications of the Declaration Signed by Pope Francis in Abu Dhabi." The American Society for the Defense of Tradition, Family and Property. Retrieved from https://www.tfp.org/theological-and-canonical-implications-of-the-declaration-signed-by-pope-francis-in-abu-dhabi/ May 20, 2021.

US job losses due to COVID-19 highest since Great Depression. University of Minnesota Center for Infectious Disease Research and Policy. Retrieved from https://www.cidrap.umn.edu/news-perspective/2020/05/us-job-losses-due-covid-19-highest-great-depression. March 26, 2021.

"Vaughn Walker." Wikipedia. Retrieved from https://en.wikipedia.org/wiki/Vaughn_Walker. April 5, 2021.

"We Were Warned: The Prophecies of St. Hildegard von Bingen." YouTube video by Return to Tradition. December 21, 2018. Retrieved from https://www.youtube.com/watch?v=MBIRupa9CHc&t=3s. May 5, 2021.

"What is coronavirus and how do we develop new treatments" The Jackson Laboratory. Retrieved from https://www.jax.org/coronavirus#. March 27, 2021.

"What is the Human Fraternity Document Signed in Abu Dhabi" The National. Retrieved from https://www.thenationalnews.com/uae/the-pope-in-the-uae/what-is-the-human-fraternity-document-signed-in-abu-dhabi-1.821882. May 20, 2021.

"What is SARS CoV-2?" Webmd.com. Retrieved from https://www.webmd.com/lung/qa/what-is-sarscov2 March 27, 2021.

Printed in the United States
by Baker & Taylor Publisher Services